BURIED ROCHESTER NEW YORK AREA

200 YEARS OF CEMETERY HISTORY

JANE HOPKINS

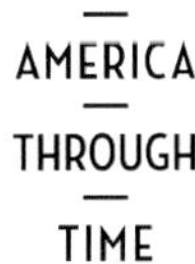

This book is dedicated to those who have gone before us and to Thomas Hopkins who helped make this book possible

AMERICA THROUGH TIME®
An imprint of SUTTON PUBLISHING INC
www.through-time.com

First published 2025

ISBN 978-1-63499-524-5

Typeset in 10pt on13pt Sabon
Printed and bound in England

Contents

Introduction 5

1 Historic Cemeteries 7

2 Modern Cemeteries 34

3 Contemporary Cemeteries 53

4 Cemetery Landscape in Context 70

Resources 93

INTRODUCTION

Cemeteries are fascinating places that reflect our history, the art of the carver, and stories of our past. Cemeteries are alive with the hopes and dreams of those buried there. They can be peaceful places for reflecting on the mystery of our life on earth.

Take the time to stroll through a cemetery, reading epitaphs, and appreciating the designs of the monuments. When I walk among the headstones and discover an interesting stone, I sometimes wonder about the person buried there. Thanks to the internet, I often can find that person's story online.

In our cemeteries lie the hopeful immigrant, the courageous wife, the cherished baby. Here is the adventurer, the young person bursting with new ideas, the venerated grandparent. And here are those who hoped for freedom to follow their religious beliefs, or to feel safe in the color of their skin. Here too are those forgotten souls who died in poverty and distress. All lie here waiting to be rediscovered by those who wander through.

When I started this project, I focused on cemetery design in the city of Rochester. But as I learned more about local history, I became intrigued by the city's ties to its surrounding area. As a result, I expanded my field of research to include the region within an hour's drive of the city.

I encourage you to seek out cemeteries along the Erie Canal, perhaps pausing at the canal museum in Lockport. Or travel in the fall along the Fruit Trail, visiting cemeteries as you sample offerings in the many local markets. You can explore the Freedom Trail from Auburn to Rochester, learning about the impact of the Underground Railroad, and the evolution of women's rights. And while exploring Genesee River Valley cemeteries to the south, take a side trip to glorious Letchworth State Park.

Buried Rochester New York Area highlights the wide variety of Rochester's cemetery experiences awaiting your exploration. The area is rich in natural beauty and history, and cemeteries serve as icing on the cake. I wish you well on your journeys through newly rediscovered buried treasures.

Rochester Area History

The Seneca Nation dominated this area for many generations before the Revolutionary War. Part of the greater Iroquois Confederacy, and known as Keepers of the Western Gate, the primary Seneca settlement flourished at Ganondagan, south of the village of Victor. Here the Seneca engaged in farming supplemented by hunting and fishing. During the seventeenth and eighteenth centuries, trading relationships with the French and British gradually developed as Europeans discovered the area's rich natural resources.

After the Revolutionary War, the destruction of many Seneca villages and a succession of treaties pushed the Seneca west and north. The Seneca never regained their strength, and they retained just a few reserved lands.

The 1790s ushered in a new era as newcomers of European descent arrived. They were determined to conquer what they saw as a wilderness and to devise new and better ways of living for themselves. The settlers brought enthusiasm and energy, expanding farming areas, and later building mills and factories. Families came filled with hope, although many found only heartbreak and failure. The new pioneers prevailed, and native American culture declined.

Life was not easy for the new arrivals. Whole families succumbed to "Genesee Fever" in Rochester's many marshy areas. Bodies had to be buried quickly, with nightly watches posted to protect graves from wolves and coyotes. I marvel at the staying power of a woman who outlived her husband and ten children. I am in awe of the persistence and back-breaking work required to clear forests for agriculture, and later to contend with marshes and rocky ledges as the Erie Canal was dug.

Rochester is located at the confluence of the Genesee River, the Erie Canal, and Lake Ontario. Early glacial activity added a fourth nearby source of water: the Finger Lakes. Abundant fresh water played a crucial role in the region's development. Initially facilitating transportation for a myriad of agricultural products, later our waters became a source of power for industry, and tourism today.

As Rochester's population increased, so too did the number and variety of our burying grounds. The area's best-known cemetery, Mount Hope, is recognized nationally as the first municipally owned garden-style cemetery, one that from its very beginning in 1838 has been open to all regardless of race, ethnicity, and religion.

Mount Hope and our many other area cemeteries convey a sense of the history of the diverse communities surrounding Rochester. One can find simple field stone markers for our early settlers, more elegant marble monuments of the Victorian period, and modern sections of individually designed granite stones for today's grandparents and parents.

The range of funerary art and epitaphs illustrates the story of a town's inhabitants, their values, and plans for future generations. They provide a sense of roots, and a focus for community pride and stability.

1
Historic Cemeteries

Burial options changed greatly during the nineteenth century in the Rochester area. Early settlers had been buried in small neighborhood burying grounds marked with field stones and wooden markers.

As the century progressed, epidemics such as cholera and typhoid filled existing cemeteries and a need arose for more spacious grounds outside the city proper. The larger towns followed Rochester's lead in developing Victorian-style garden cemeteries, featuring family plots with headstones of neoclassical design in marble. Obelisks sat side by side with individually designed headstones. Situated in an area of hills and valleys with winding roads and ponds, these park-like cemeteries were places that attracted people for strolls and picnics while visiting departed family members. Smaller town cemeteries added obelisks and Victorian designs to their offerings while continuing to be very accessible to visitors.

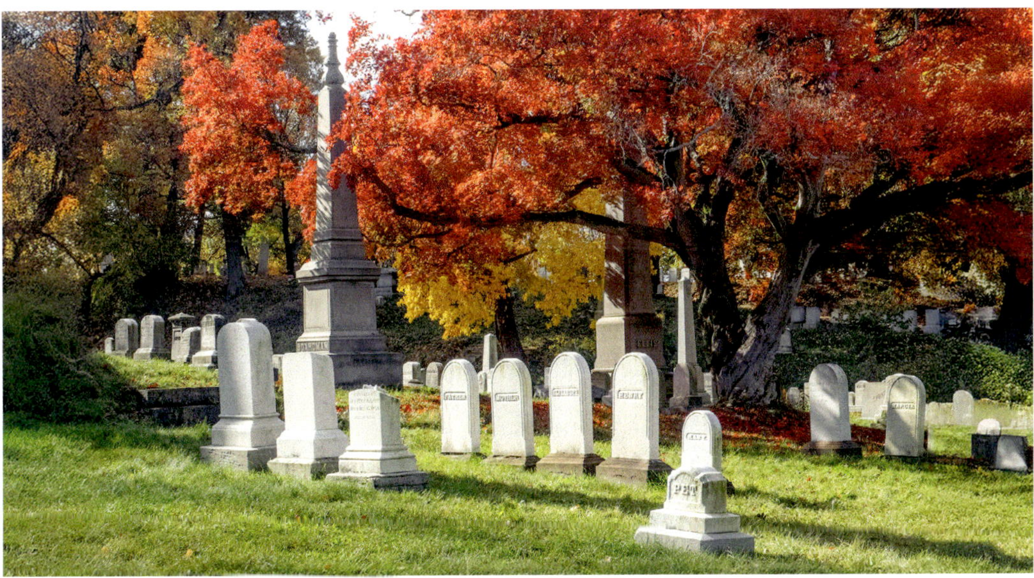

The marble headstones shine in the sunlight at Mount Hope Cemetery. Imagine what these old burying grounds must have been when they were new!

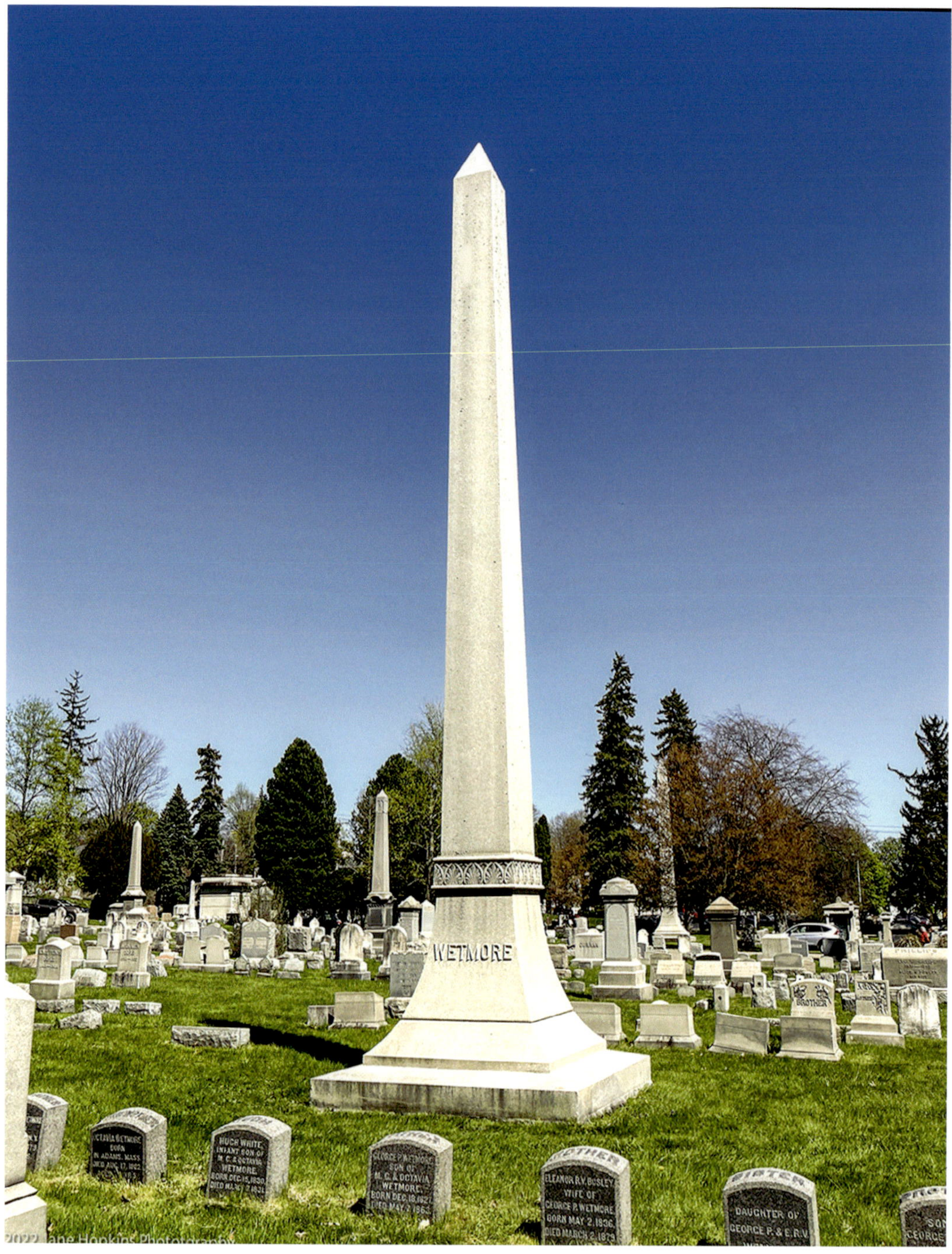

A grand obelisk watches over a panoply of early headstones at Mount Hope cemetery, each representing a precious life that has become an integral part of our history.

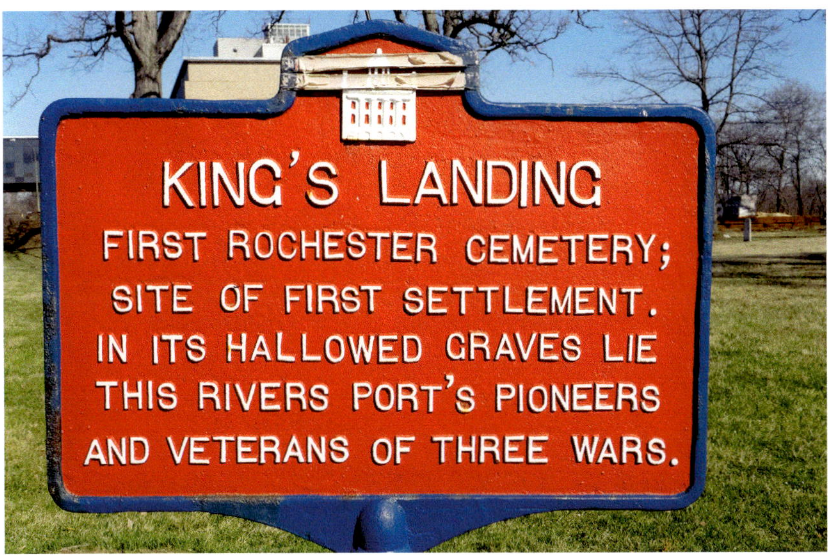

The first official burying ground in what is now Rochester was created in 1798 for the King's Landing community, named for pioneer settler Gideon King. After "Genesee Fever" (likely typhoid or malaria) carried away most of the King family, the Hannaford family arrived, renaming it Hannaford's Landing. Today a few stones remain in this cemetery across from Kodak Park, reminding us of these hardy souls.

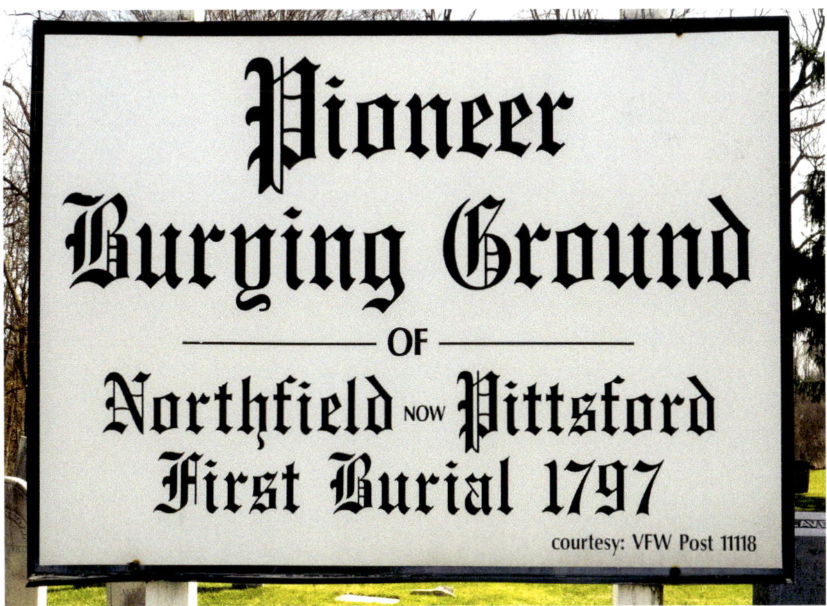

The town of Northfield (later Pittsford) was created in 1789 by Revolutionary War soldiers Simon and Israel Stone. They laid out the Pioneer Burying Ground when they drew up their plans for the town. In this well-maintained cemetery, look for the pioneer families of Sarah and Stephen Lusk and Dorothy and Col. Caleb Hopkins.

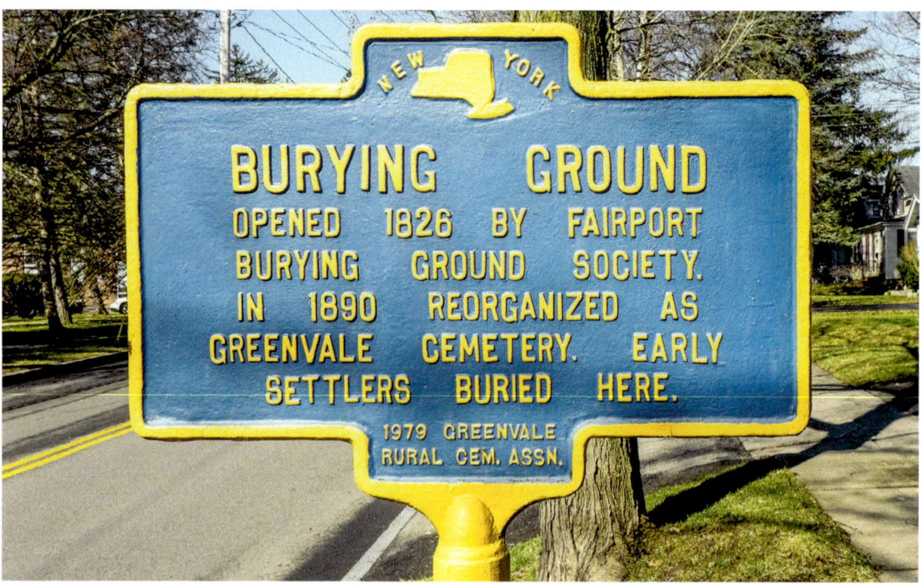

The town of Fairport originated when land was drained for the construction of the Erie Canal. It quickly became a bustling port, and later an important railroad hub, as the local fruit processing and packing industry grew. Greenvale Cemetery was established near the canal in 1825–26.

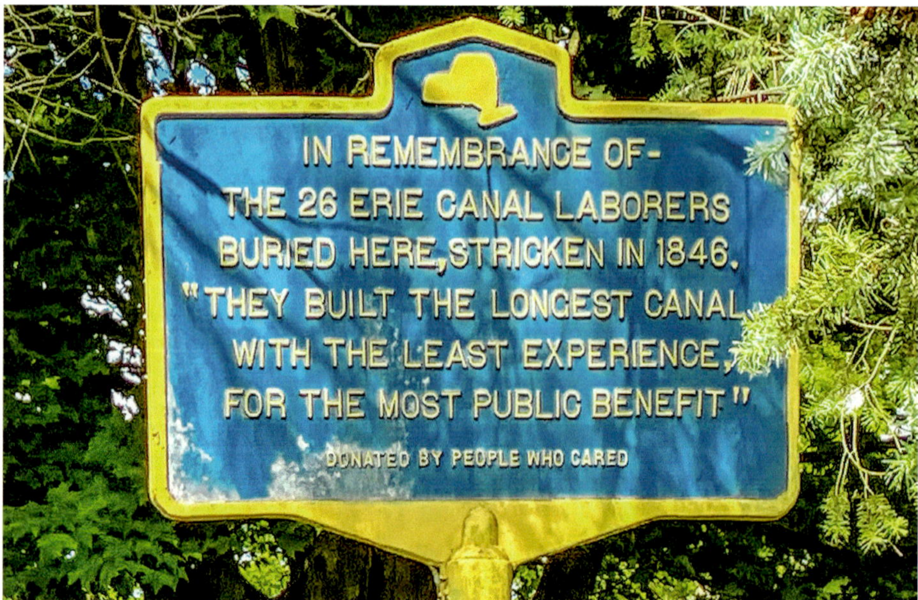

Unsung canal workers braved marshes, muck, mosquitos, and unending lifting of heavy loads in this remarkable initiative. Most deaths went unrecorded far from home. Wayneport's Union Burying Ground, Macedon, honors a group of Irish laborers who died of smallpox when working on the canal in 1846. They are buried together here in an unmarked grave.

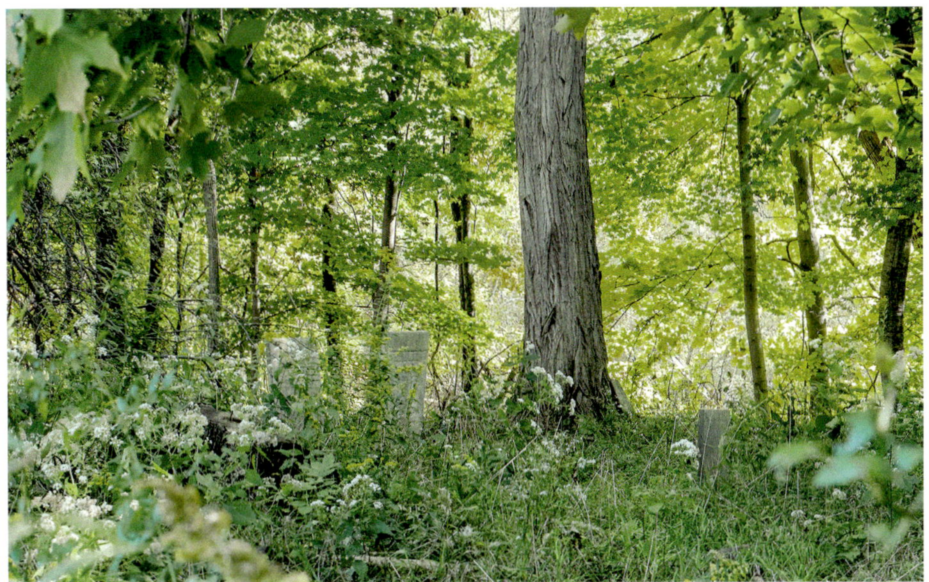

Established in 1816, Davis Cemetery, Ontario, sits along Lake Road and is thought to be the oldest cemetery in the village. A sign recognizing War of 1812 veteran Jesse Gage highlights this cemetery. Though now overgrown, several headstones are still standing, including that of Gage's wife, Mercy, mother of their ten children. It takes devoted neighbors and organizations to keep these historic sites cleared and the stones repaired.

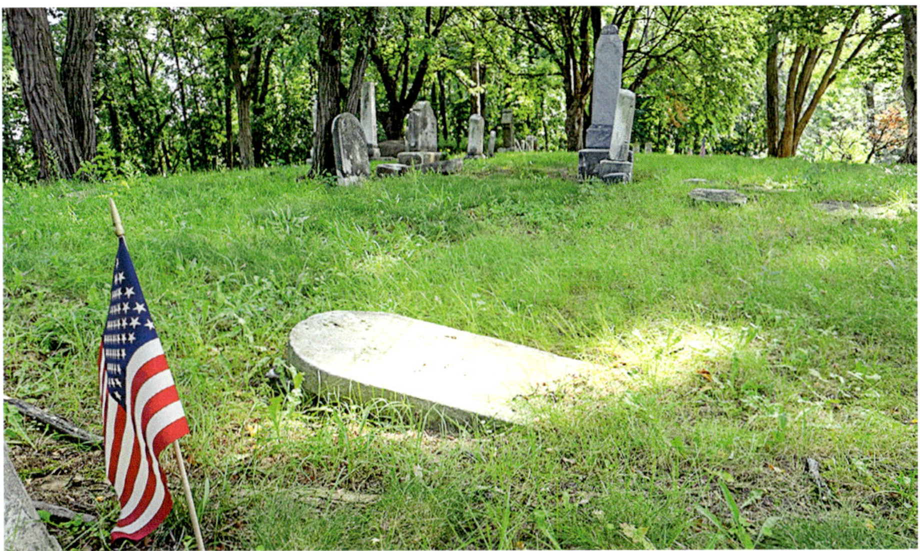

When its first European settlers arrived, the Rochester area was part of a vast forest crossed by an ancient Seneca Indian Trail from Canandaigua to the Genesee River. Hooker Cemetery in Irondequoit borders that trail, renamed Merchant's Road by the settlers. Now compressed between Route 104 and Saint Ann's Home, the cemetery has lost many of its stones to time and development.

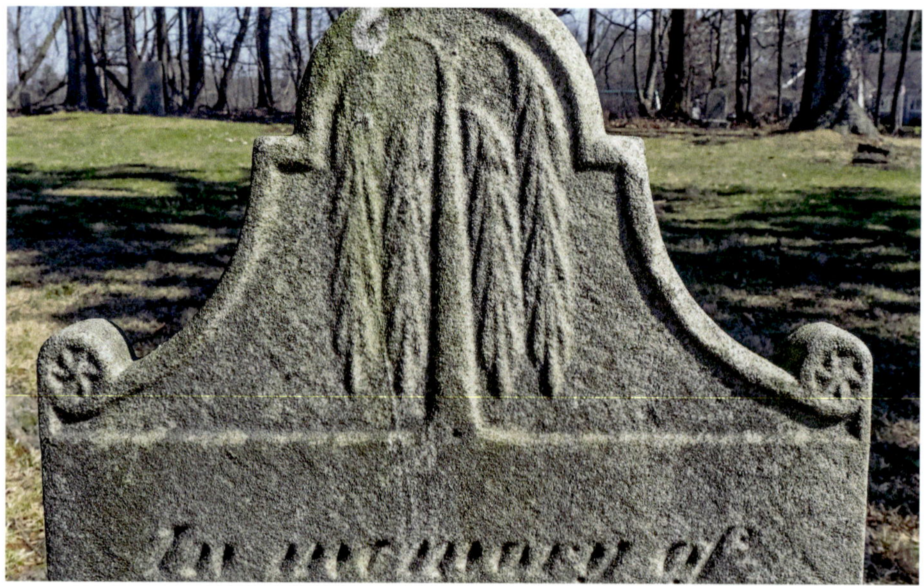

As families arrived from New England and Pennsylvania, they may have had access to headstone designs available "back home." This style depicting the willow tree (representing grief) resembles many seen up and down the East Coast of the U.S. The stone for Mathew De Garmo is similar in shape and style to those for his family of eight buried between 1822 and 1836 at Old Mendon Cemetery, Mendon.

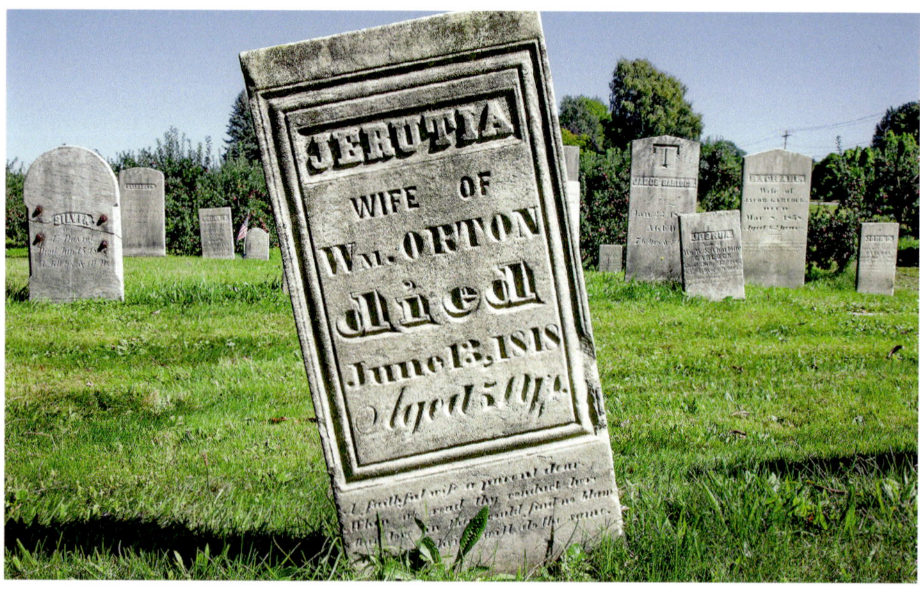

The large rectangular stone for Jerutia Orton at Bushnell Burying Ground, Sodus, is deeply carved and uses a variety of fonts not often seen in this area. This type of stone using differing fonts is called an alphabet stone. The Orton epitaph reads: "A faithful wife, a parent dear; When we read thy conduct here; Our love in thee would find no blame; And love divine will do the same."

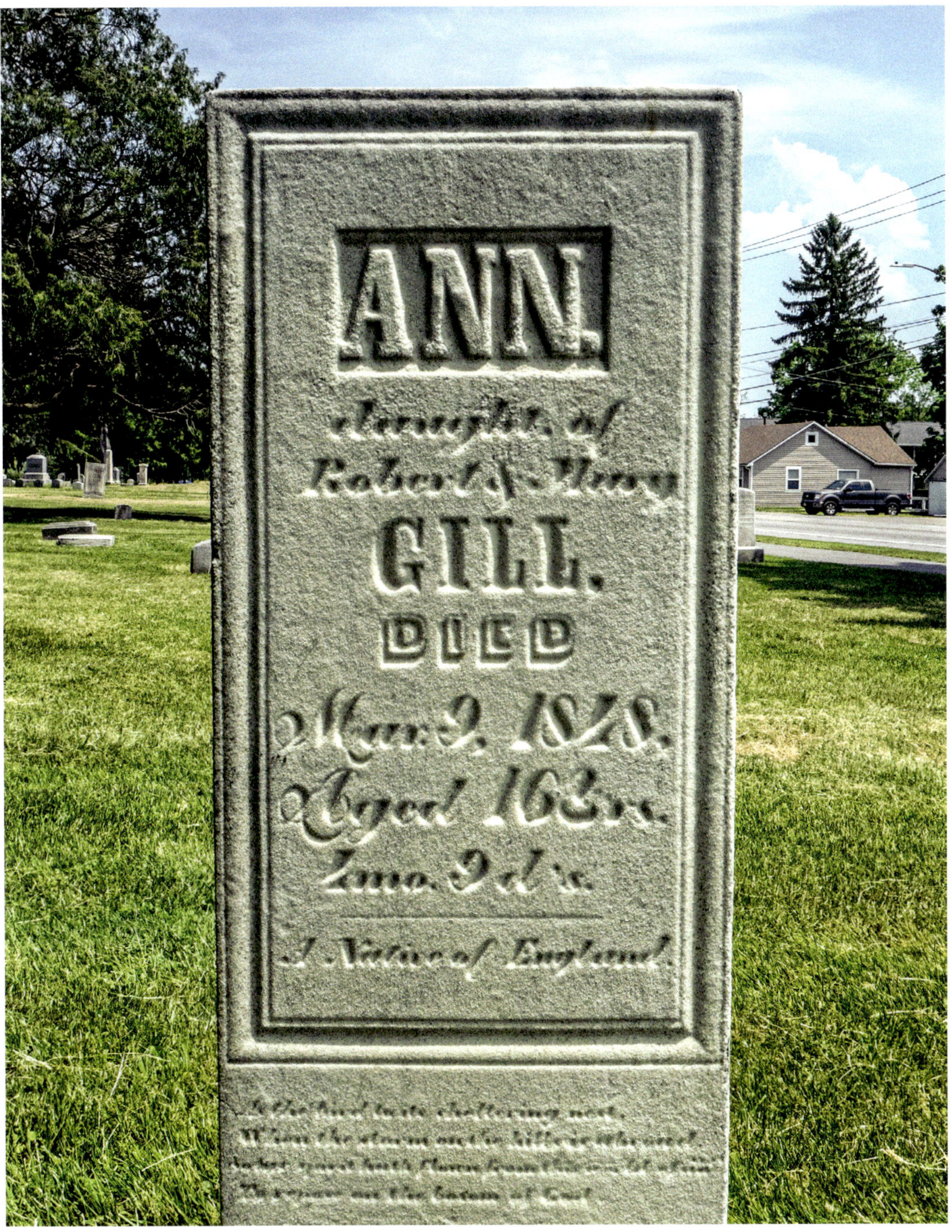

Ann Gill was buried with her family in Temple Hill Cemetery, Geneseo. Established in 1807, this burying ground has a large variety of early to mid-nineteenth-century monuments. The pictured marble alphabet stone is in remarkably good condition, reflecting the masterly workmanship of its carving. As is typical with this style, an epitaph is inscribed at the bottom. Jerutia and Ann died the same year. I wonder if a brochure was published that year detailing "alphabet" fonts

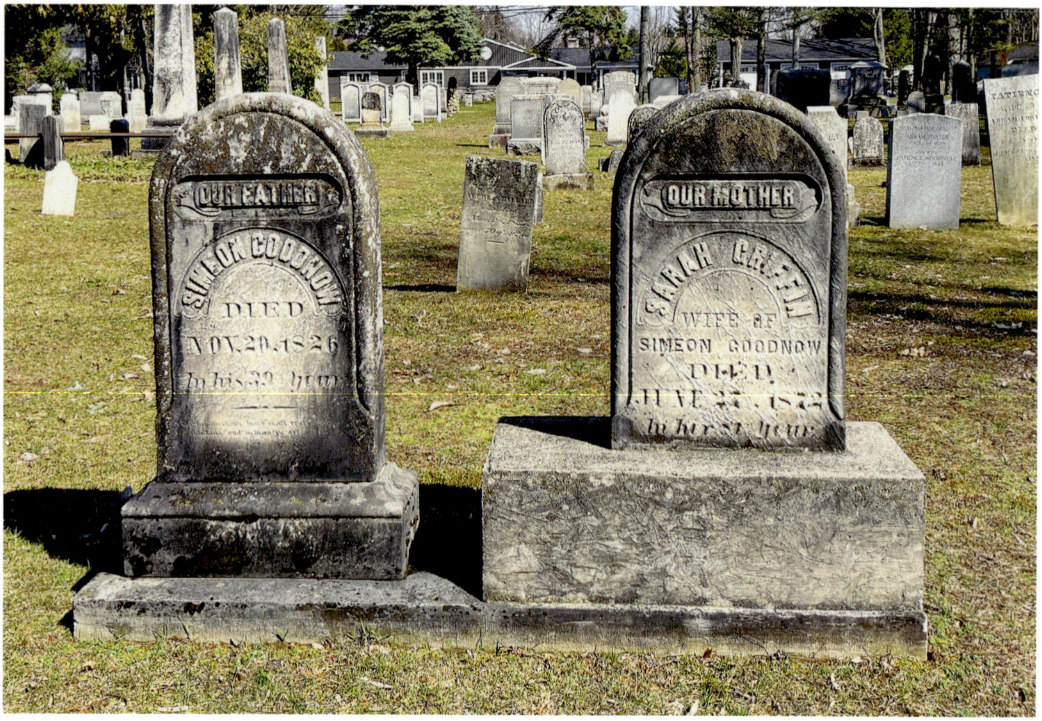

Lives are not always lived in orderly fashion. Simeon Goodnow died in 1826 at age thirty-nine. His wife, Sarah, died forty-six years later in 1872. Someone has rescued her broken stone in a thoughtful way by re-setting it on a higher base. These headstones at Webster Union Cemetery are typical examples of the rounded top-style limestone/marble used in the Rochester area throughout the early to mid-1800s.

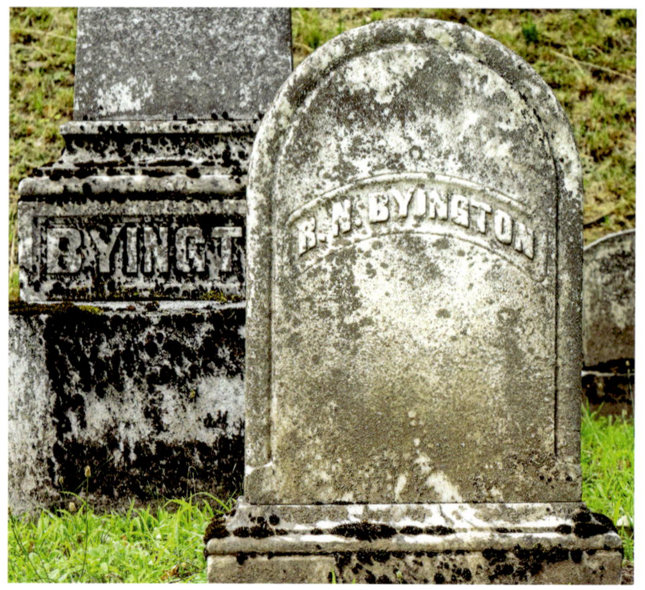

These stones at Mt. Albion Cemetery were created during a time when stone carvers were in short supply. Headstones were shaped at the quarry as "blanks." They arrived requiring minimal carving onsite. By the time the Erie Canal was finished, Lockport was quarrying high-quality headstones and obelisks, easily transported by canal to its neighbors further east. Stones and monuments in these cemeteries of 200 years ago take on their own patina with age.

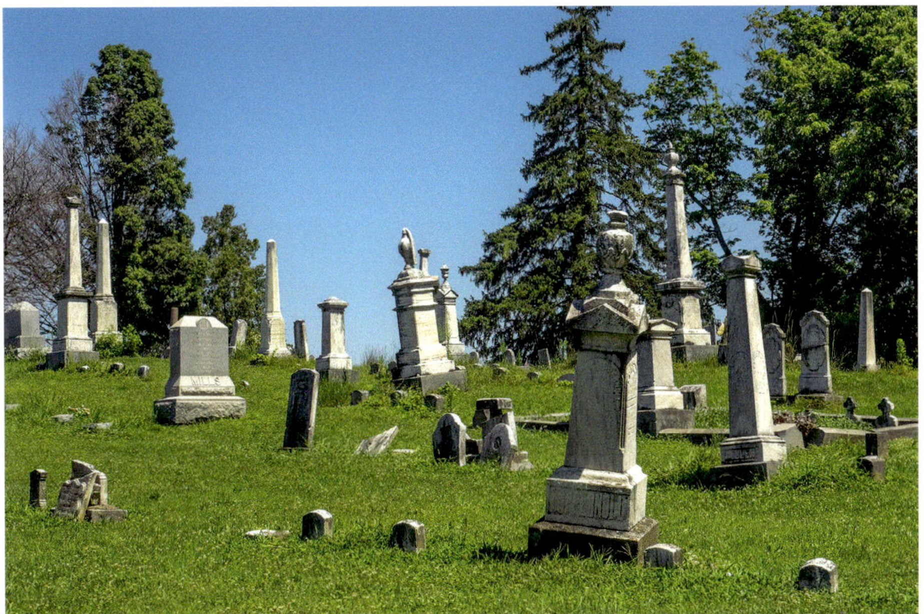

Union Hill Cemetery, Cato, was established in 1802 on a hill overlooking neighboring agricultural fields. Various headstone shapes are intermixed with obelisks, creating a handsome vista of heights and styles. The monuments lean here and there as if talking to each other. I look forward to stopping by whenever I drive in that direction.

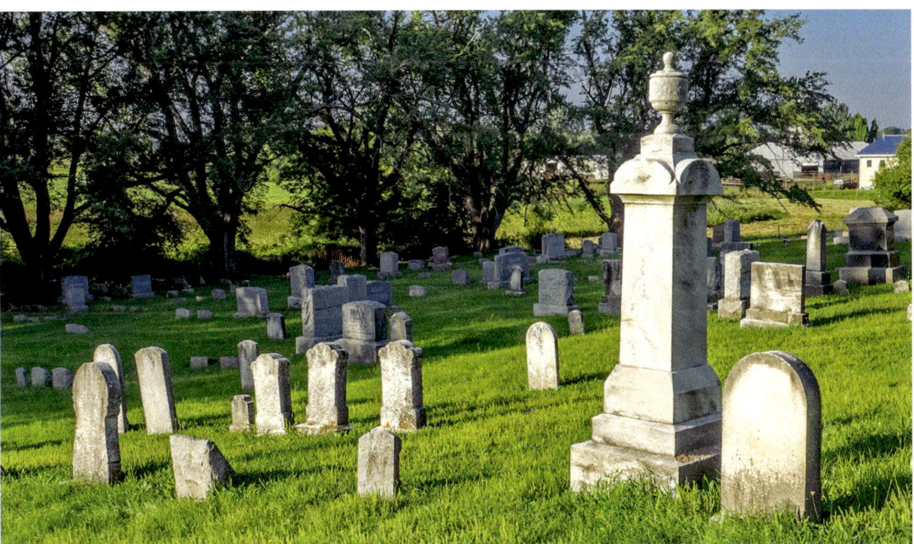

The Rochester area abounds with cemeteries in its small towns and villages such as Union Hill Cemetery, Webster. A first reaction to many upstate cemeteries can be that they are all alike—old marble stones, a few obelisks, many not readable. However, as you look more carefully, you may recognize a name, wonder about the relationships in a family group, or spot a little gem in a style not common to the area.

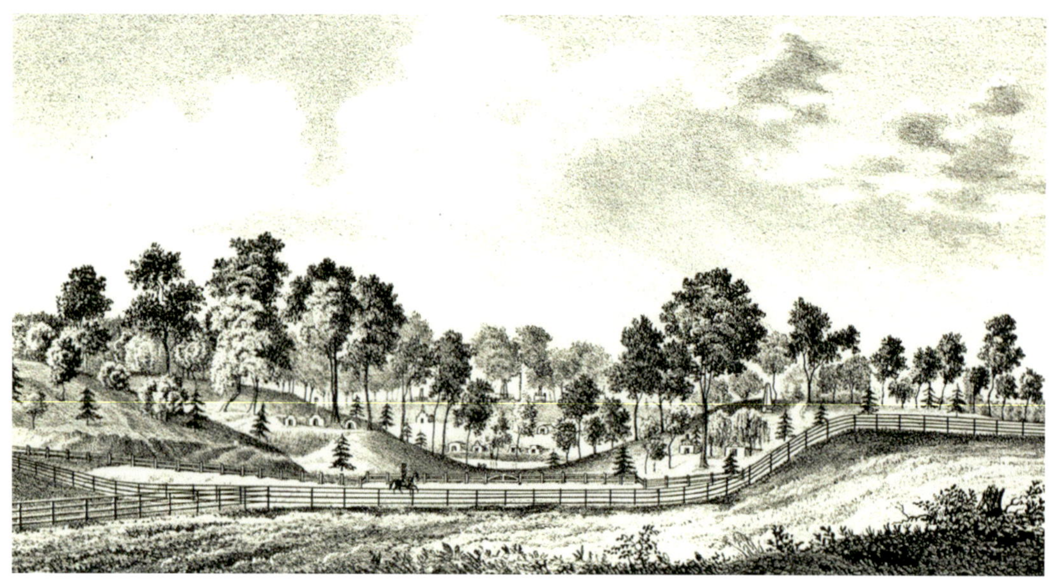

After the opening of the Erie Canal, the city of Rochester grew rapidly. Other towns along the canal followed suit. As the population increased and epidemics took hold, the garden cemetery was born. Mount Hope was created at the edge of town in a sylvan setting with an undulating landscape. These early images depict the lovely natural home chosen for the nation's first municipal garden cemetery, which from the outset has been open to all. Mount Hope is shown above in 1838 as it was naturally endowed with trees, hilly and flat terrain, and lovely vistas over the surrounding landscape. Below is a view of its north gate in 1877. (*Images from The History of Monroe County by W. H. McIntosh, courtesy of the Local History Division of the Rochester Central Library*)

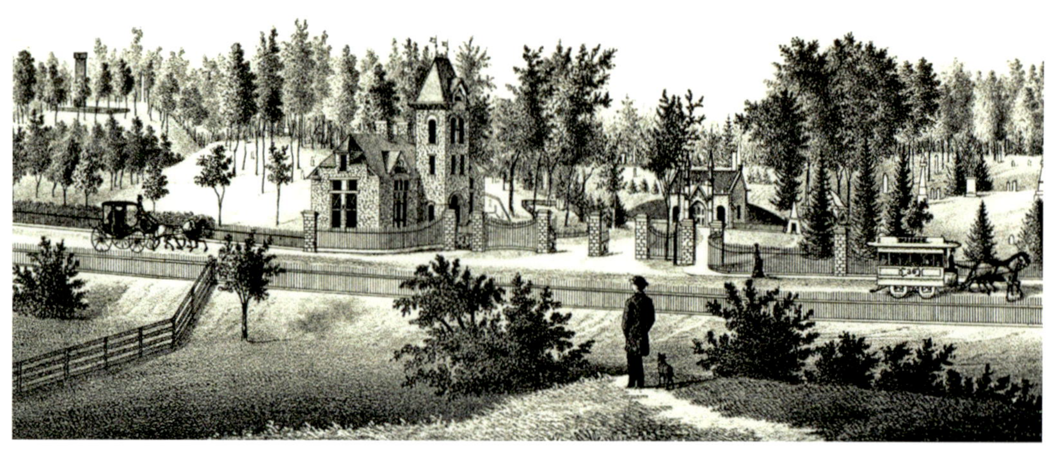

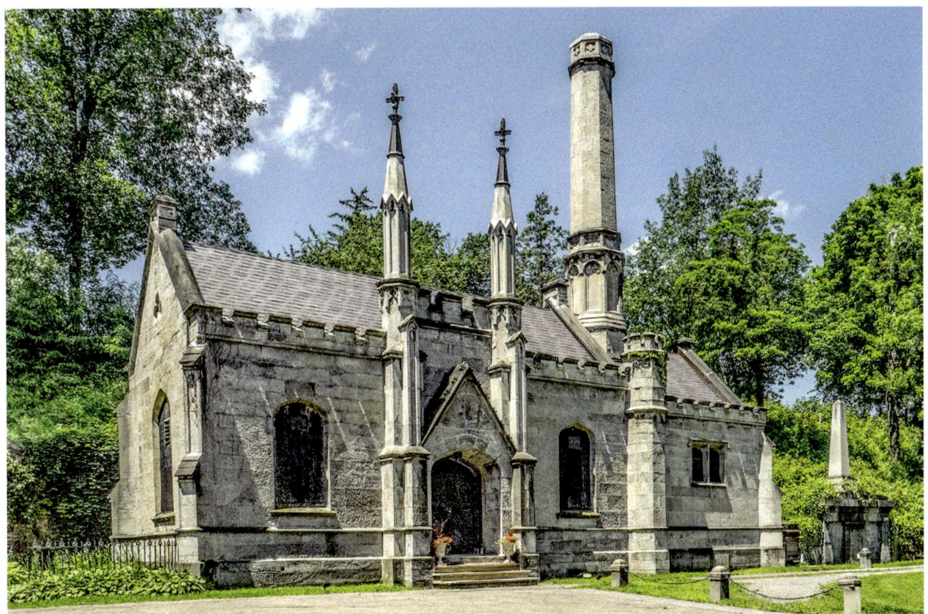

Elaborate chapels and entrance buildings welcomed the public to newly created Victorian garden cemeteries. The Old Chapel at Mount Hope Cemetery was constructed of Lockport limestone in 1862. Designed by Henry Searle and Son, the interior had walnut paneling and was adorned with stained glass windows. A 30-foot receiving vault extended into the hillside behind.

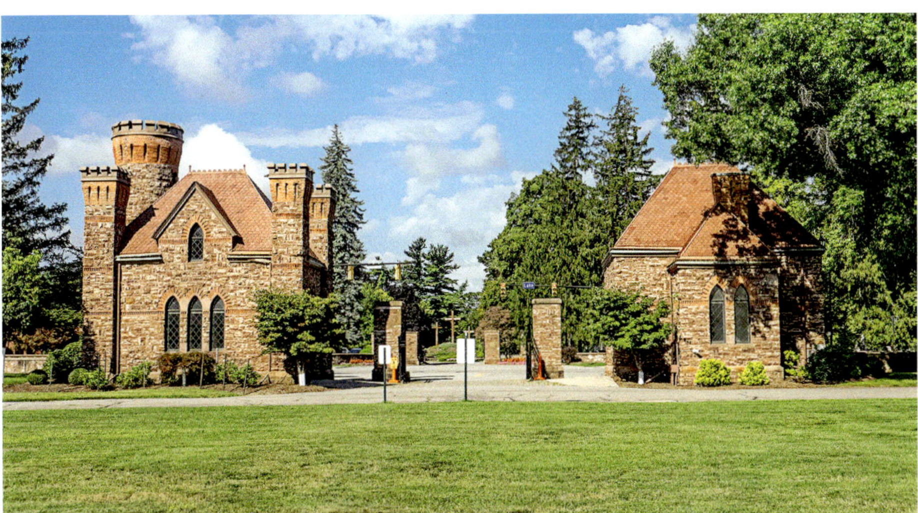

Holy Sepulchre Cemetery established a second major garden cemetery in Rochester in 1872 under the guidance of Rochester's first bishop, Bernard J. McQuaid. Two gatehouses at the east entrance were designed as waiting areas for visitors using the Lake Avenue trolley line. Situated on the Genesee River, the cemetery shares a border with Riverside, a third garden-style cemetery, created to serve people on the north side of the city.

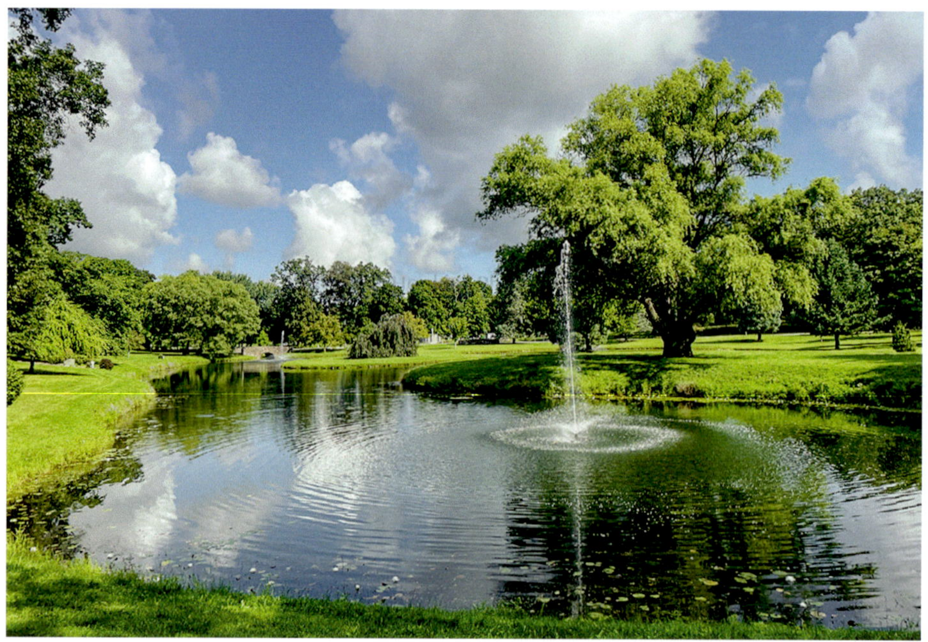

A hallmark of garden cemetery design is beautiful scenery designed for quiet reflection. This pond at Holy Sepulchre Cemetery is stunning on a summer day. Surrounded by headstones, it provides a tranquil place of remembrance in a lovely setting away from the bustle of the city.

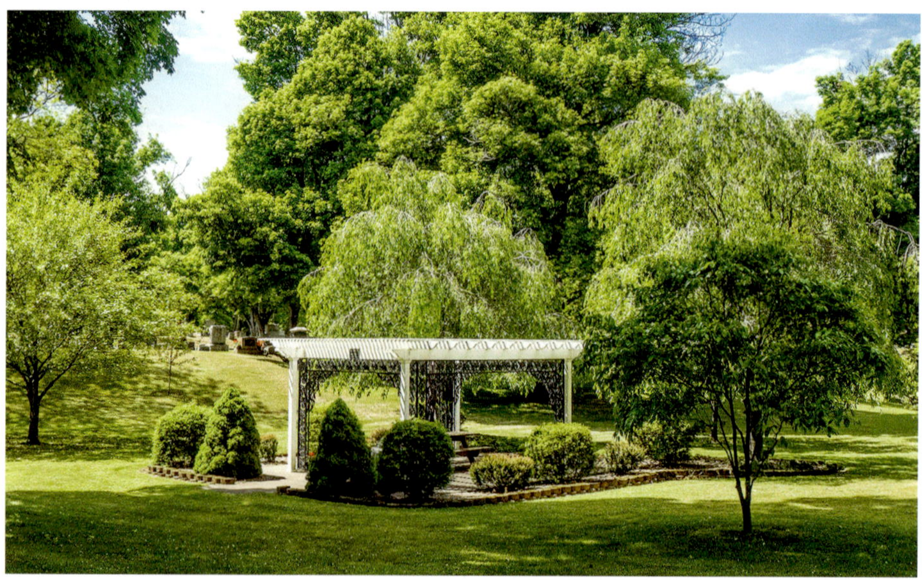

At Mount Albion Cemetery, Albion, another quiet oasis is reminiscent of the Victorian gardens that were models for these nineteenth-century cemeteries. Trees of various types and heights form a backdrop, with shrubs protecting this secluded spot.

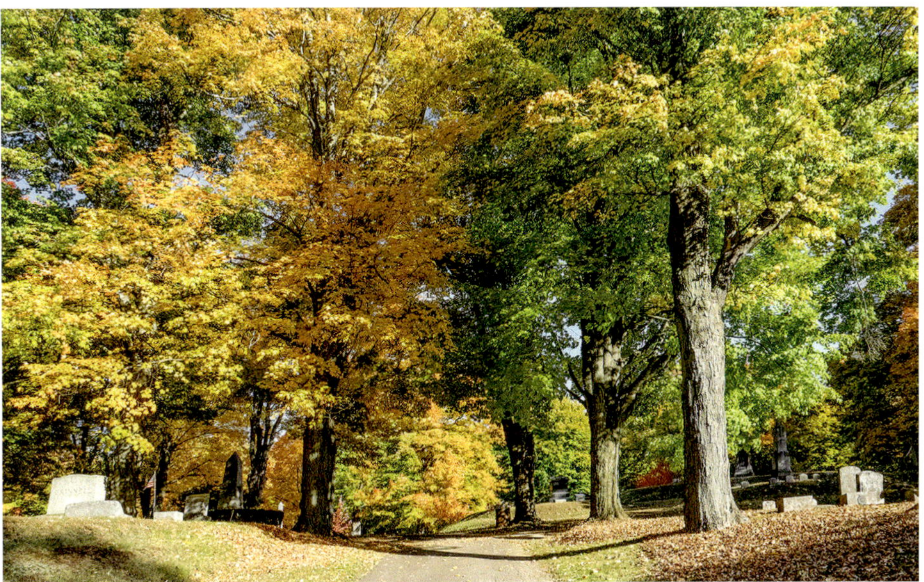

Many Rochester area garden cemeteries take advantage of dramatic landscapes created by the receding glaciers of long ago. Trees thrive along the roadside as it winds up steep terraces to the Soldiers and Sailors monument at the top of a glacial drumlin (cone-shaped hill) in Mount Albion Cemetery, Albion.

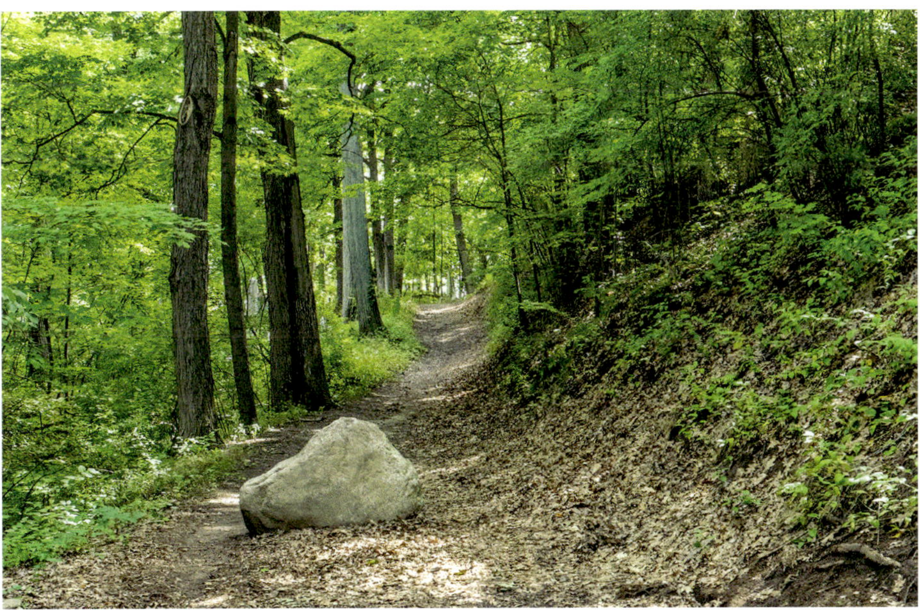

Hiking paths lead to vistas of trees and monuments at Mount Hope Cemetery. The view changes as you round each bend in the trail. Area cemeteries are favorite places for geology students to study the varying topography of eskers (ridges), drumlins, and kettles (depressions).

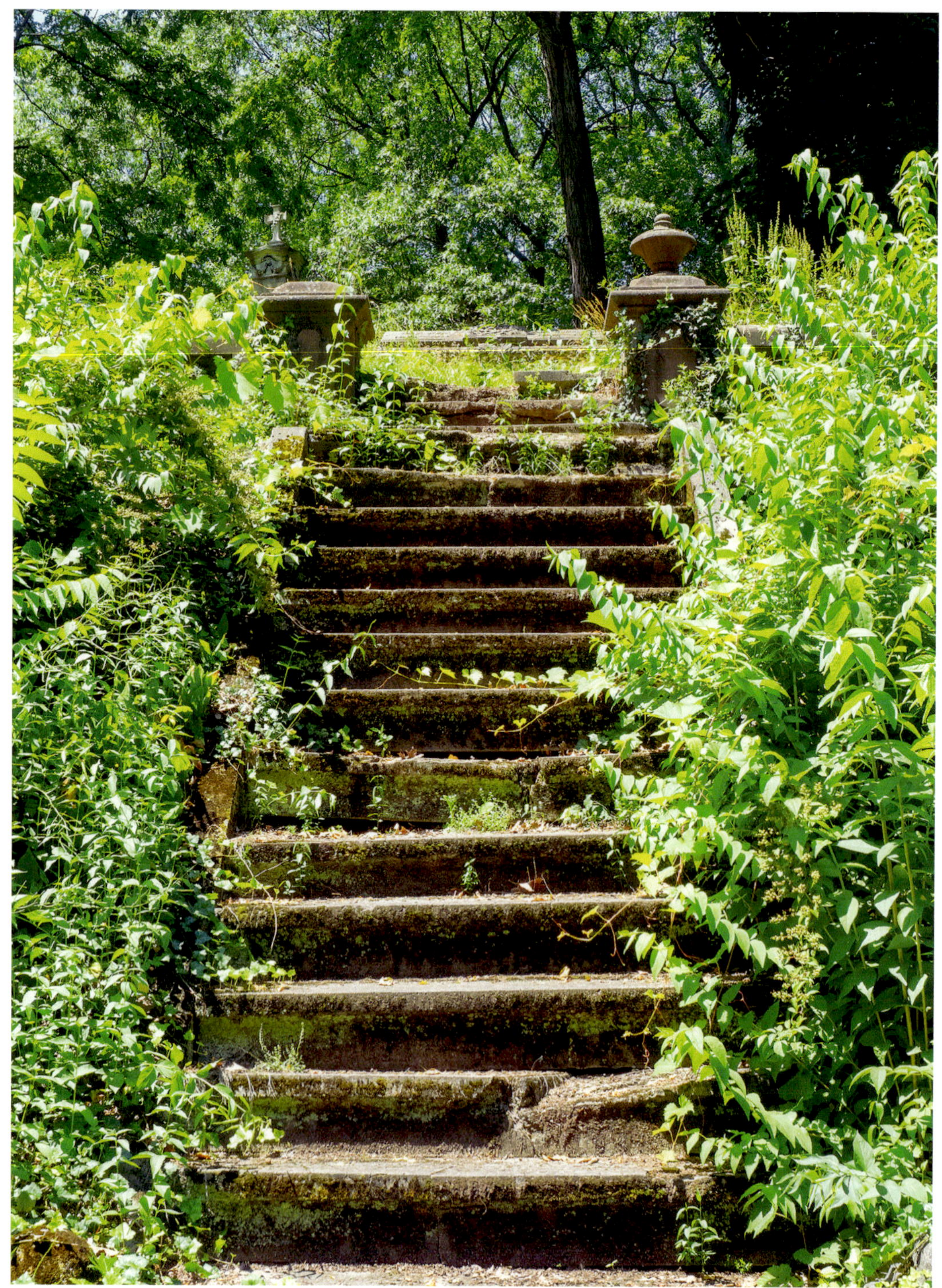

This stairway at Mount Hope leads to a remote family plot. Such pathways contribute an air of mystery to wandering through our area garden cemeteries.

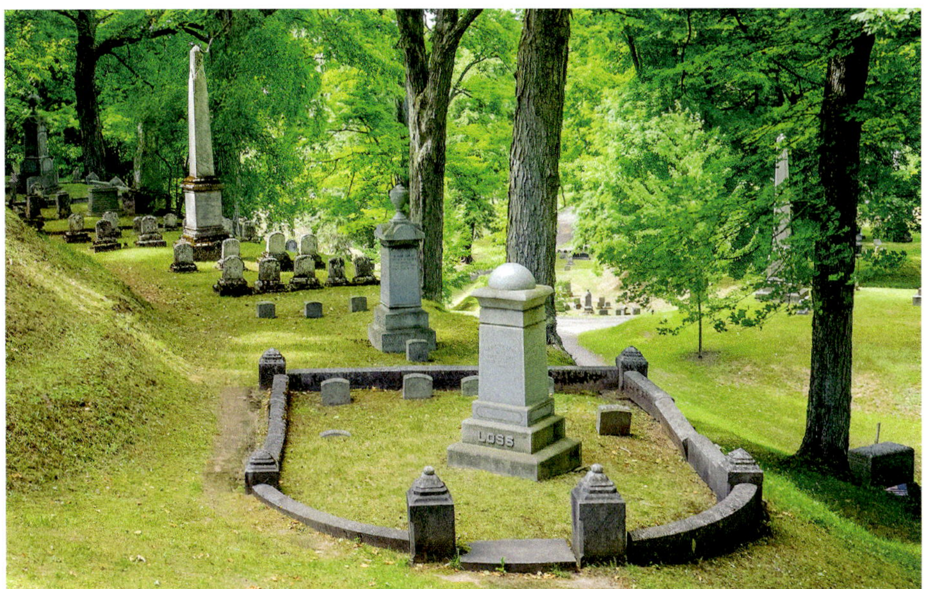

The steep drumlin at Mount Albion Cemetery necessitated terracing to accommodate the monuments. Terraces were just wide enough to hold a large monument surrounded by smaller ones for family members. At a time when families were large and often stayed in the local area, family burial plots were a popular option. Eliza and Lewis Loss are buried here with their six children.

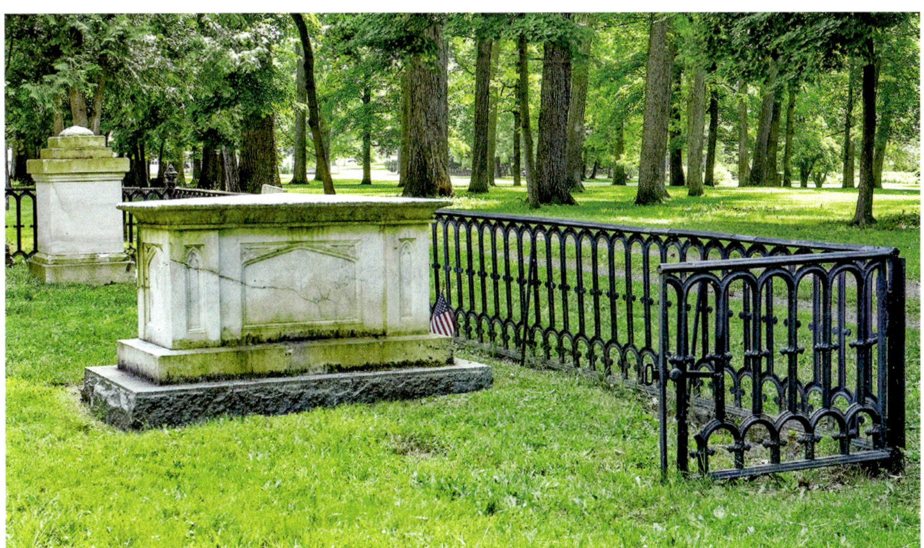

Further south, the valley of the Genesee is wide and fertile, with some of the best agricultural land in New York. James Wadsworth arrived in Geneseo in 1790 and is buried with his family at Temple Hill Cemetery, created in 1843. The handsome wrought-iron fence surrounding the family plot is typical of the period. Few are left today since many have fallen into disrepair, or the metal used for the war effort in WWI.

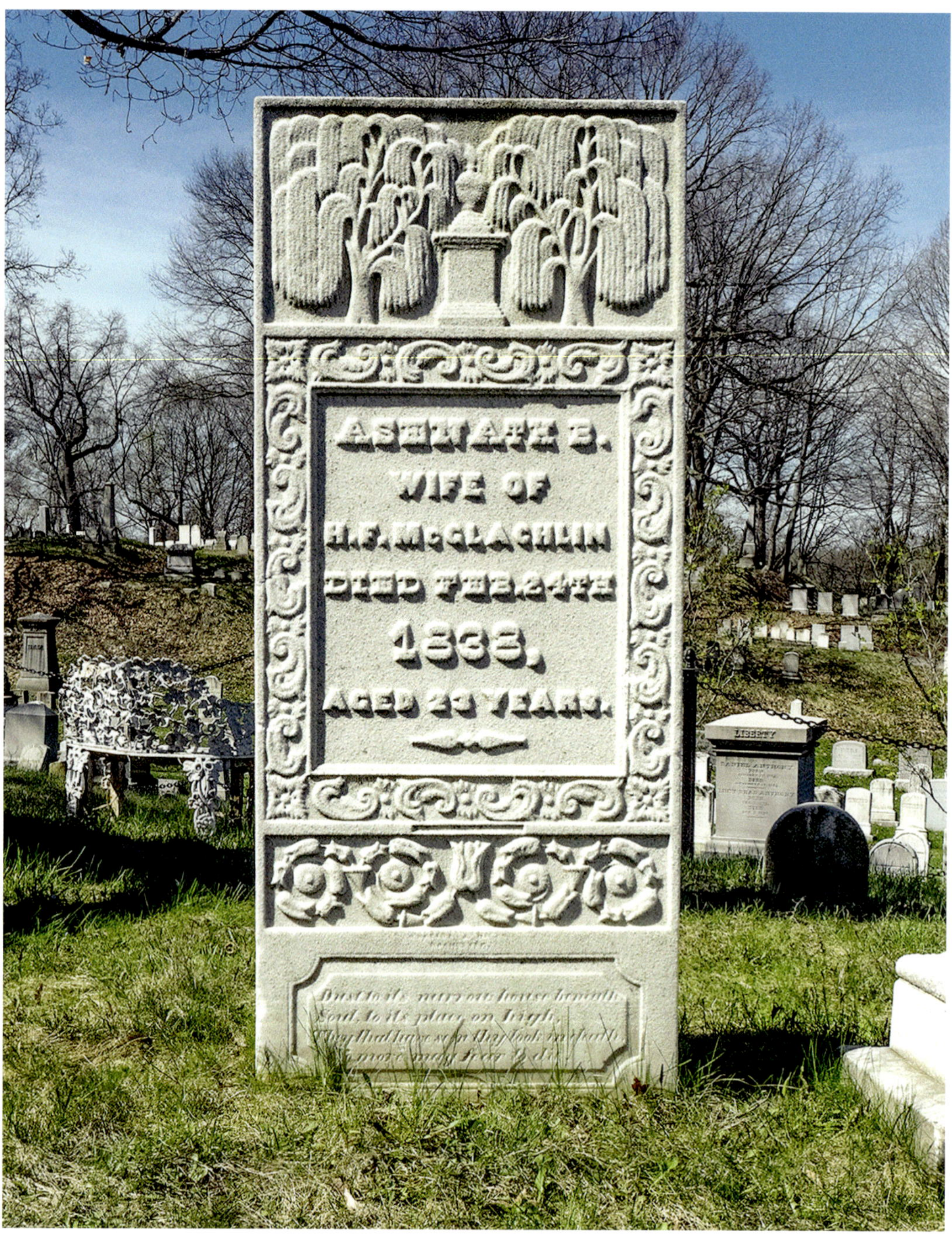

Asenath McGlachlin died at age twenty-two in 1838. Hers was one of the first burials in Mount Hope Cemetery. The headstone's elegant double willow and urn design is also the logo of Friends of Mount Hope, a volunteer group responsible for restoration work at the cemetery. The urn is a classical funerary symbol used by the Romans for cremated remains; the weeping willow represents grief, sorrow and mourning. These motifs were a hallmark of Victorian-era headstones in the mid-1800s.

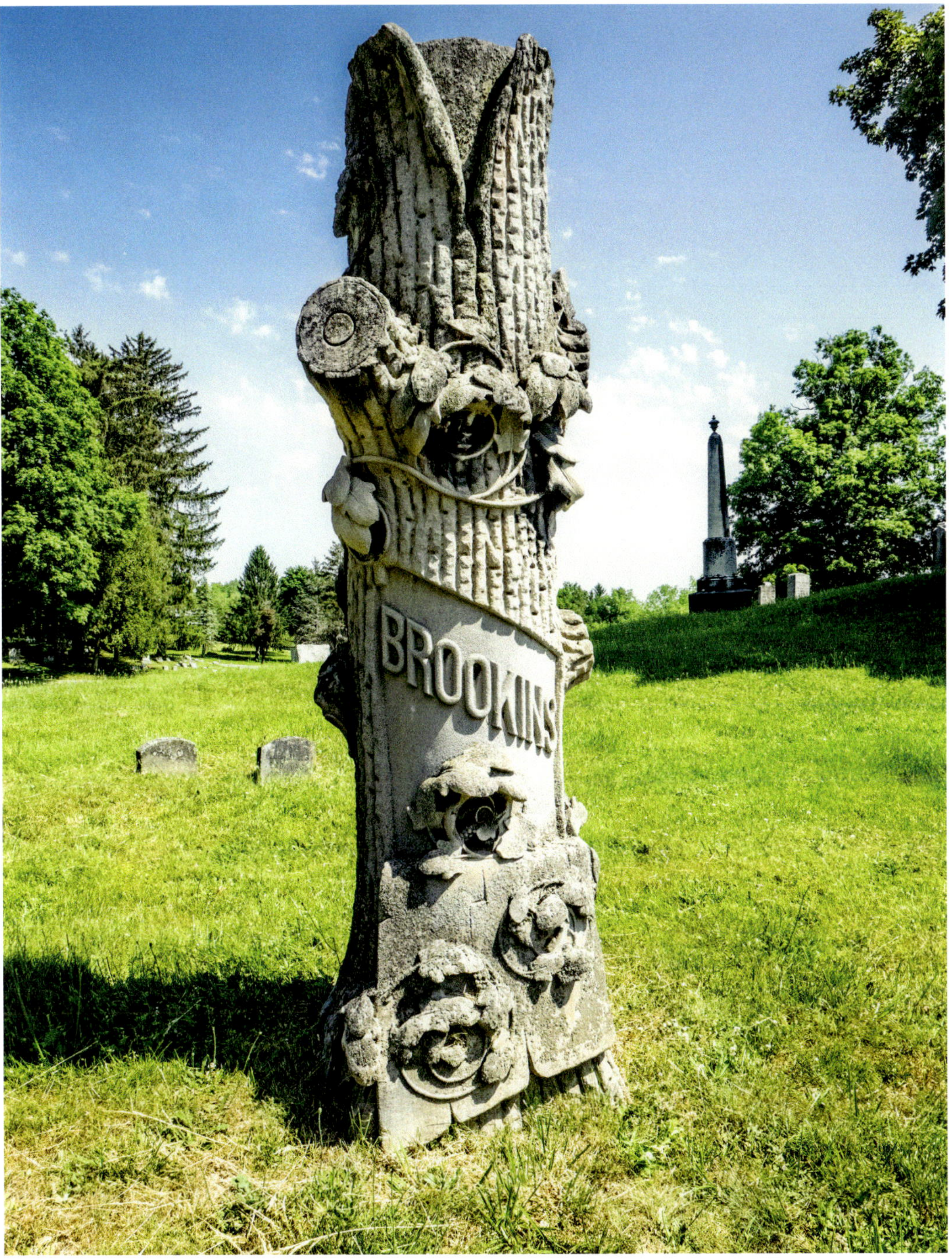

This memorial for the family of Ellen and James Brookins at Mount Morris Cemetery, is a fine example of tree stump monuments popular in the late 1800s. "Stumpies" became the symbol of the fraternal organization Woodmen of the World. The tree stump signifies a life cut short and an appreciation of nature.

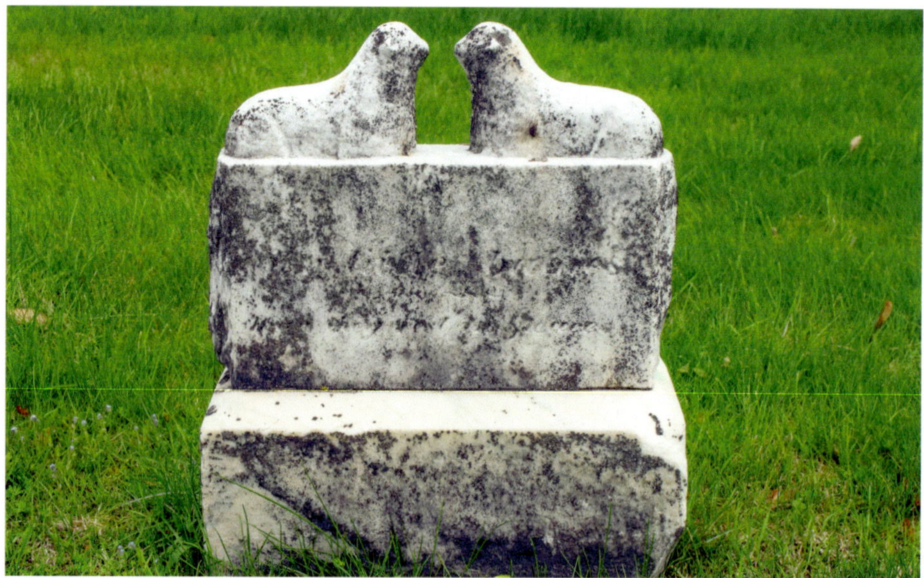

It always is sobering to see a child's headstone because it represents the dashing of hopes and dreams for a young life. Lambs have been a common symbol for a child's death since the 1850s. They represent purity and innocence. Holy Sepulchre Cemetery, Rochester, has a large children's section from the 1800s. This double lamb headstone may indicate twins.

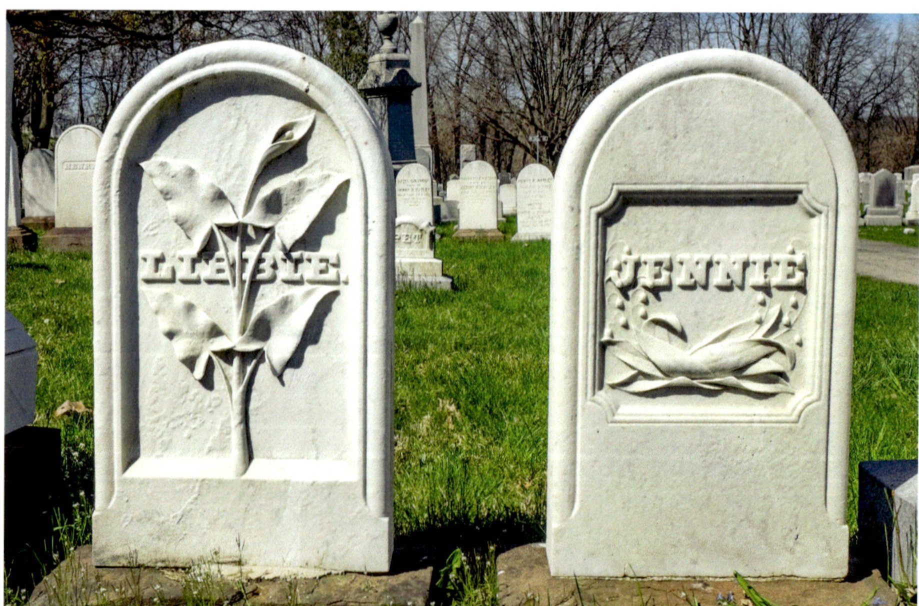

These two lovely stones for sisters caught my eye at Mount Hope Cemetery because of their unique design. Researching the family on Find a Grave, I found Jennie and Libbie Copeland. Their mother, Maria, had ten children and outlived them all, as well as her husband. I wonder how she survived such losses.

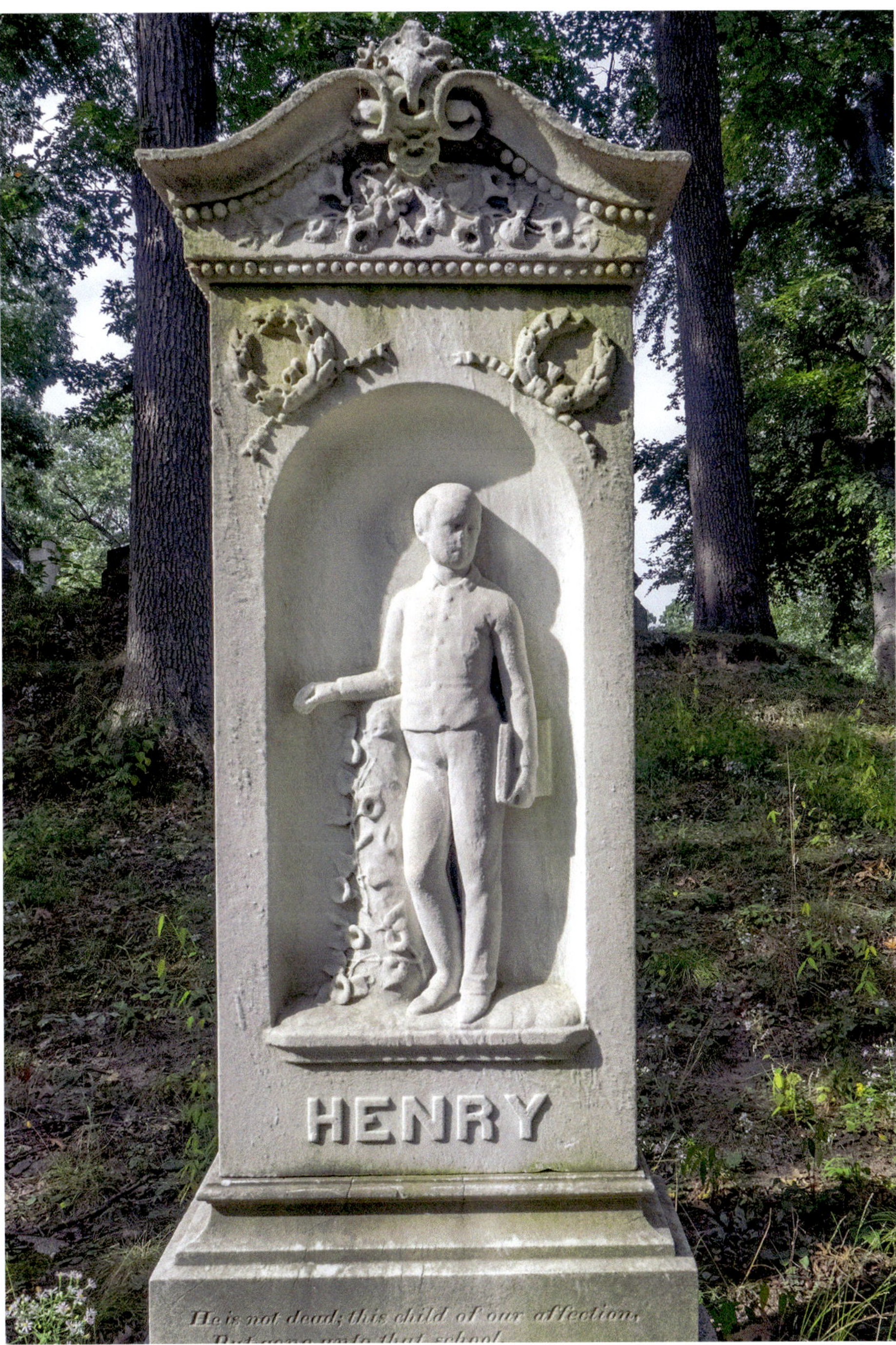

This lifelike statue of Henry Selden at Mount Hope Cemetery tugs at the heart. When he was thirteen years old, Henry drowned while his father was teaching him how to swim in Irondequoit Bay. The monument was created by R. E. Launitz, who chose a tree stump as a worthy symbol. Henry is buried beside his parents and his only brother who also died young.

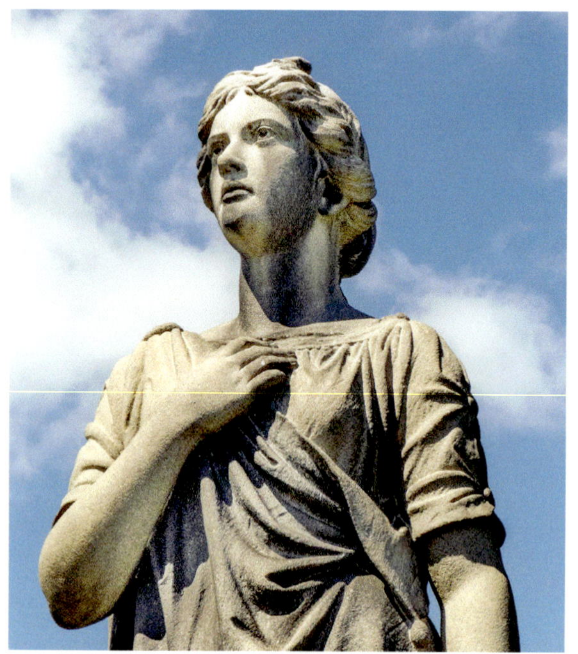

There are many beautiful statues in Rochester area garden cemeteries. The figure above at Mount Hope Cemetery represents the allegorical figure of Hope. Dressed in classical robes, she holds an anchor symbolizing faith and hope for an eternal life. Her face is turned heavenward, comforting those left behind, knowing that their loved one's soul has entered eternity.

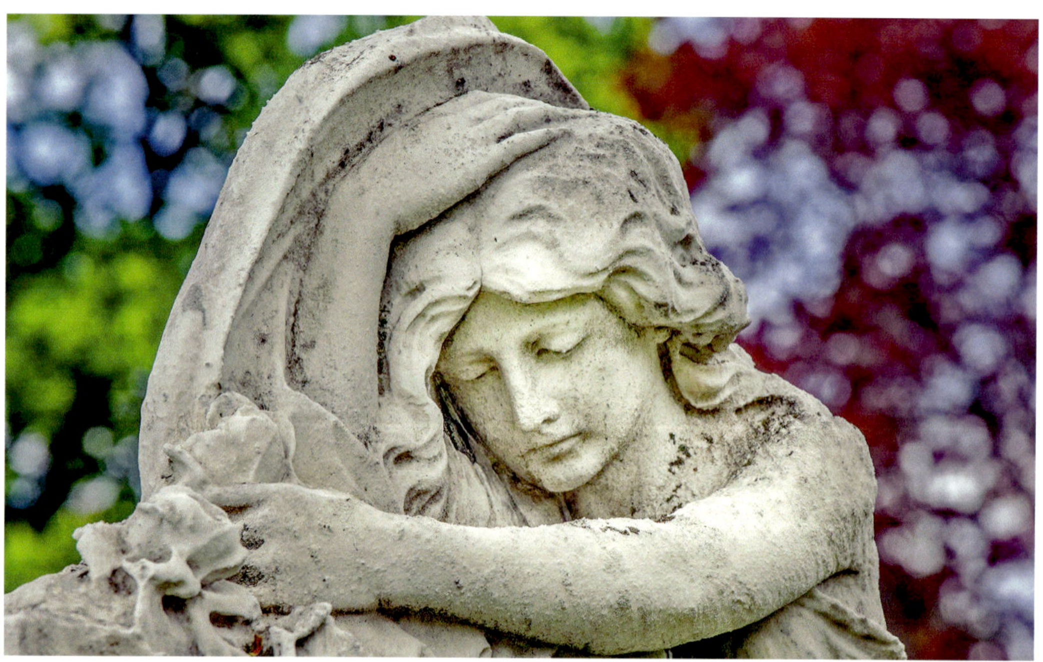

This figure at Holy Sepulchre Cemetery, Rochester, represents grief and appears in many forms in Victorian cemeteries. The statue has a gentle, timeless presence watching over the grave.

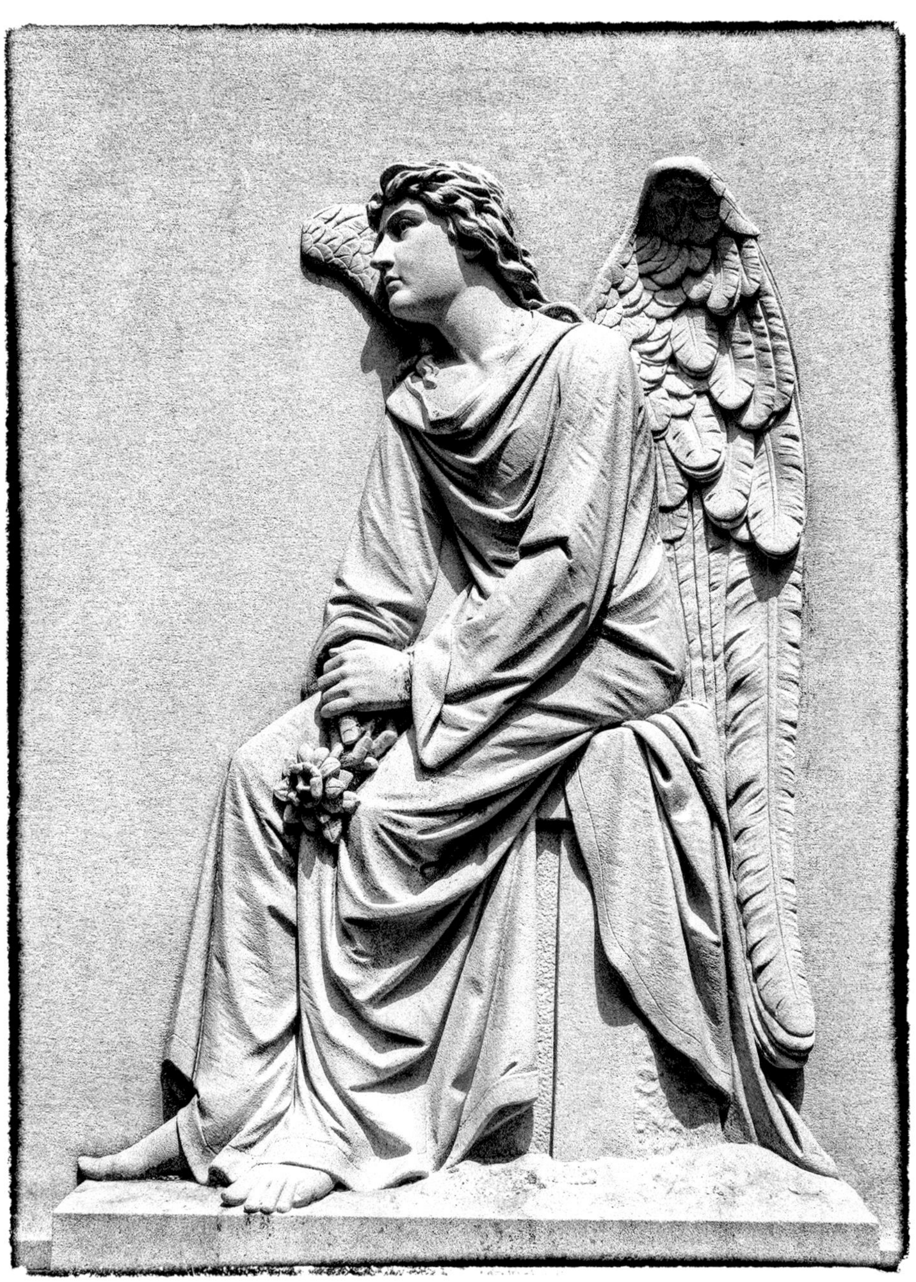

This thoughtful, patient angel looks off in the distance, holding a bouquet of flowers. Perhaps he is there supporting the Corwin family's grief when son George died at age five in 1851. Reading the history of the Corwin family, I was surprised to learn that when the Corwin farm was sold in 1894, part of it became the Browncroft neighborhood in Rochester where I walked my dog on Corwin Road 100 years later.

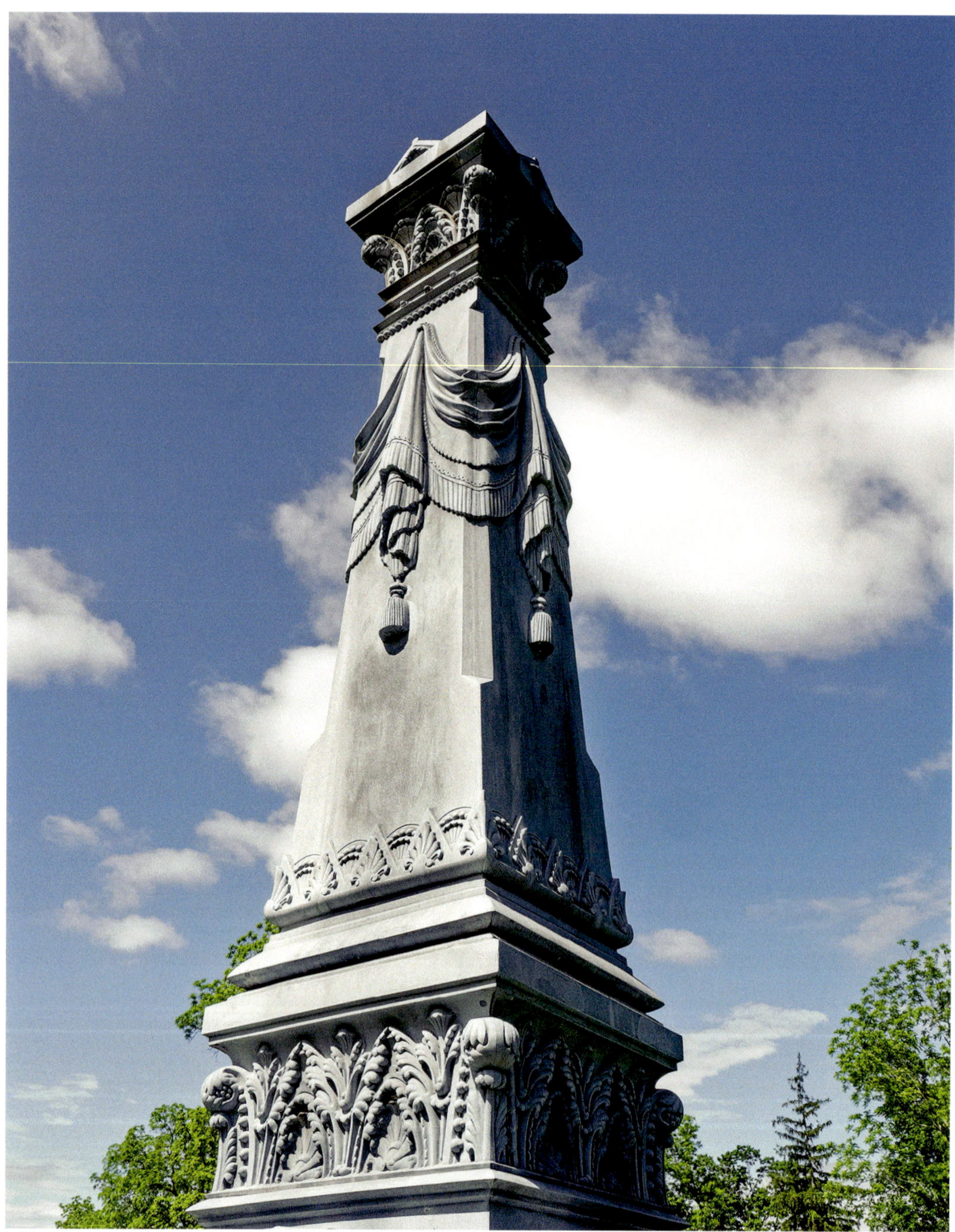

Elizabeth and Jacob Shoemaker and daughter are honored by a grand zinc monument at Restvale Cemetery, Seneca Falls. Also called white bronze, these monuments could be custom ordered from the Connecticut Bronze Company or ordered through the Sears catalog. Wandering through cemeteries in the Rochester area, it is fun to find a "zinkie" with its metallic blue color and hollow sound when tapped. Look for the name plates created for each family member as needed.

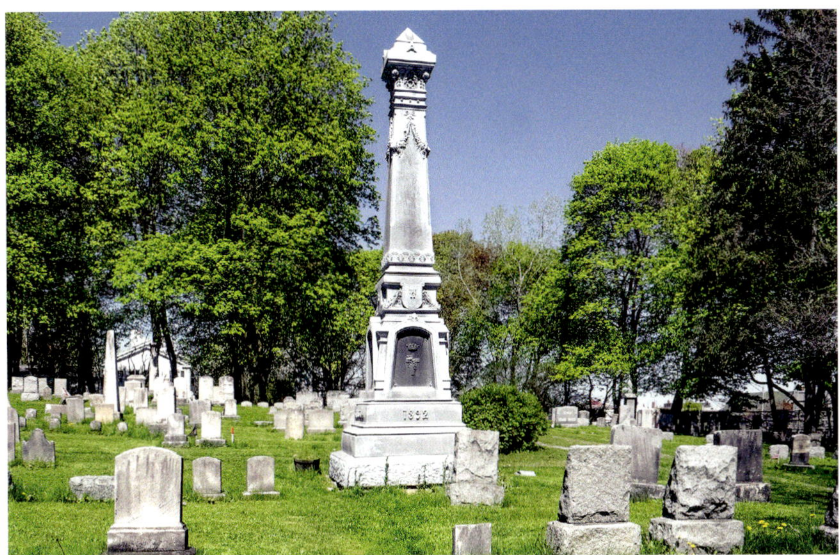

Brighton Cemetery, founded in 1821, is home to a 25-foot-tall white bronze monument dedicated to the Cynthia and Schyler Watson family. This cemetery is an historic gem hemmed in by modern development. Originally a tranquil setting at the edge of the Erie Canal, it now is wedged between the I-490/I-590 interchange and a residential neighborhood.

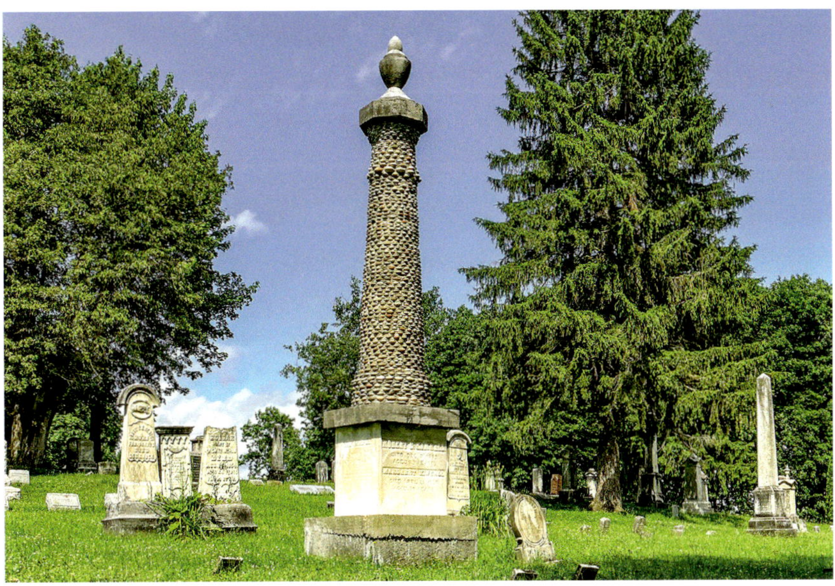

Meridian Cemetery on Route 370 in Cato is the site of a stunning cobblestone monument honoring the family of Margaret and Robert Kimball. Dating back to about 1840 and recently restored, it follows the tradition of cobblestone architecture in this region. The cemetery, just down the road from the Union Hill Cemetery, is a mix of wonderful old shapes and designs from the mid-1800s.

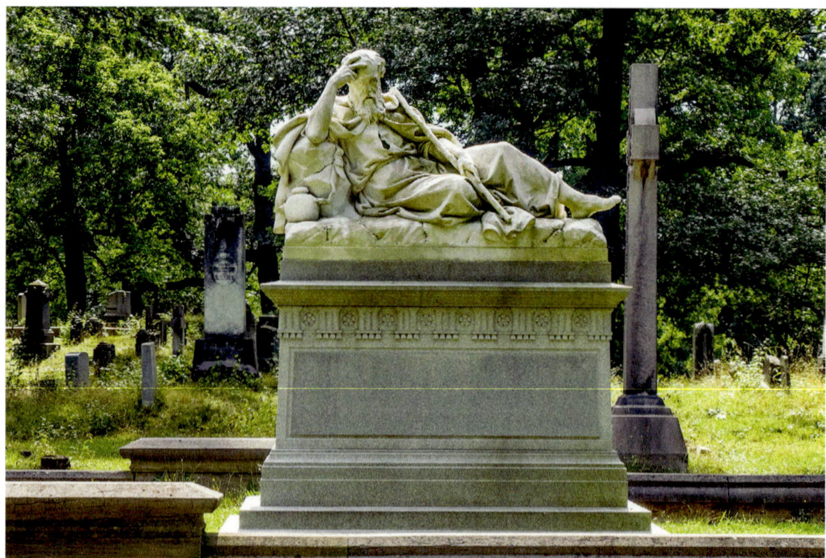

Mount Hope has some famous sculptures among its tree-lined hills. "The Weary Pilgrim" was sculpted by Nicola Cantalamessa-Papotti for Hannah and Aaron Erickson and their eight children. The family founded the Rochester Institute for the Deaf following the struggles of their deaf son. The statue was shipped from Italy and placed upon a grand base designed by Claude Bragdon.

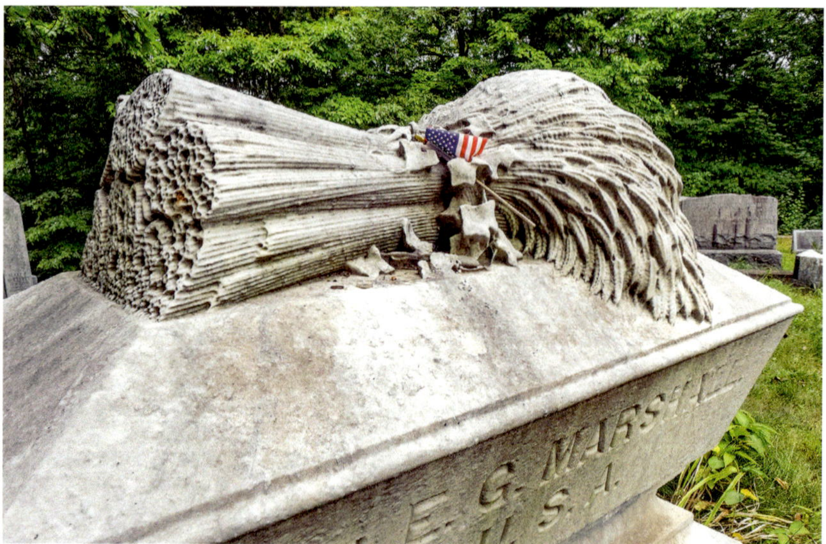

Viola Erickson, daughter of Hannah and Aaron, married General E. G. Marshall. She died at age twenty-eight of diphtheria a month after the death of her one-year-old son, Aaron, of the same disease. Her husband, who survived fighting and imprisonment during the Civil War, died ten years later at fifty-four. The sheaf of wheat that adorns the family grave represents God's harvest. It is wrapped in ivy that represents undying love.

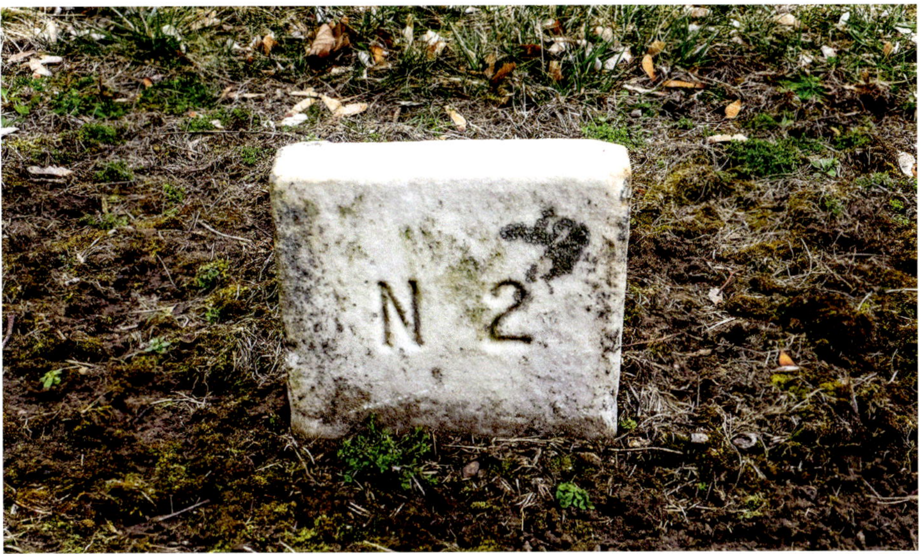

Amid grand monuments in the area's cemeteries are resting places of those less fortunate, buried with little fuss in unmarked graves. This person does have a monument in the Ontario County Poorhouse Cemetery, Hopewell. He or she has lost their identity, however, having become Inmate Number 2, an indication of the attitude of the time towards the mentally ill and the indigent.

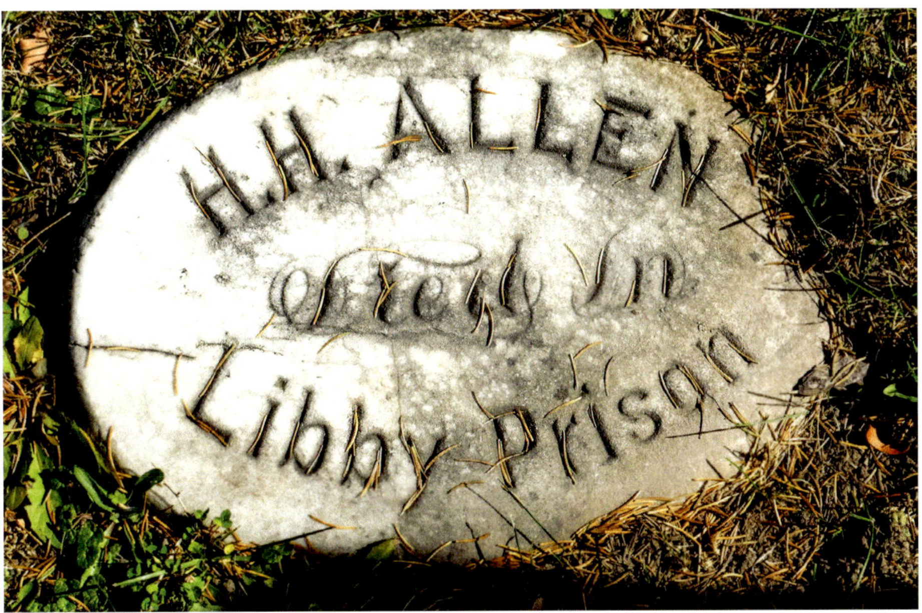

An inmate of a different kind is honored by a small plaque among the many grand markers at Newark Cemetery. H. H. Allen died in Libby Prison, Richmond, VA, during the Civil War. That infamous prison, formerly a warehouse, housed 24,000 Union soldiers during the war, many of whom died of starvation and disease. The plaque may be a cenotaph—a representative marker for a person buried elsewhere—in this case probably Richmond.

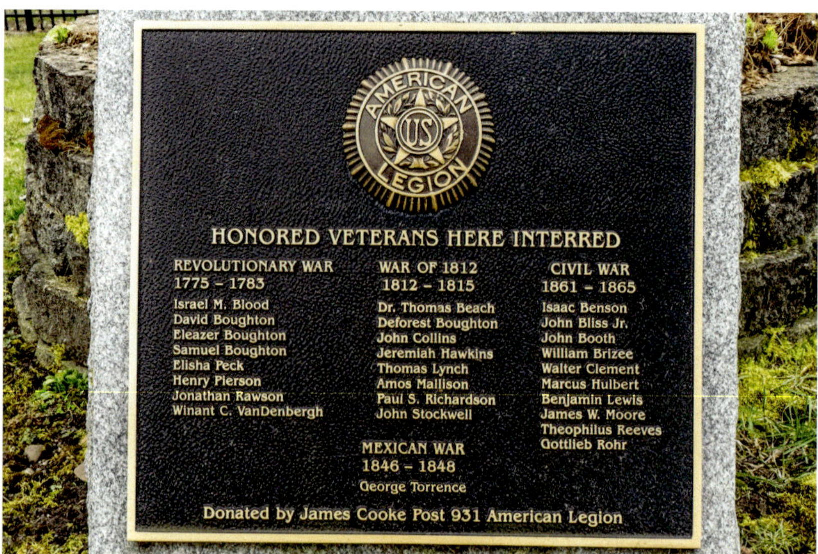

Created in 1810, the small Victor Village Cemetery is hidden behind the Methodist Church and next to the railroad tracks in the center of town. Throughout the 1800s it witnessed the burials of its veterans of the Revolutionary War, War of 1812, Mexican War, and the Civil War.

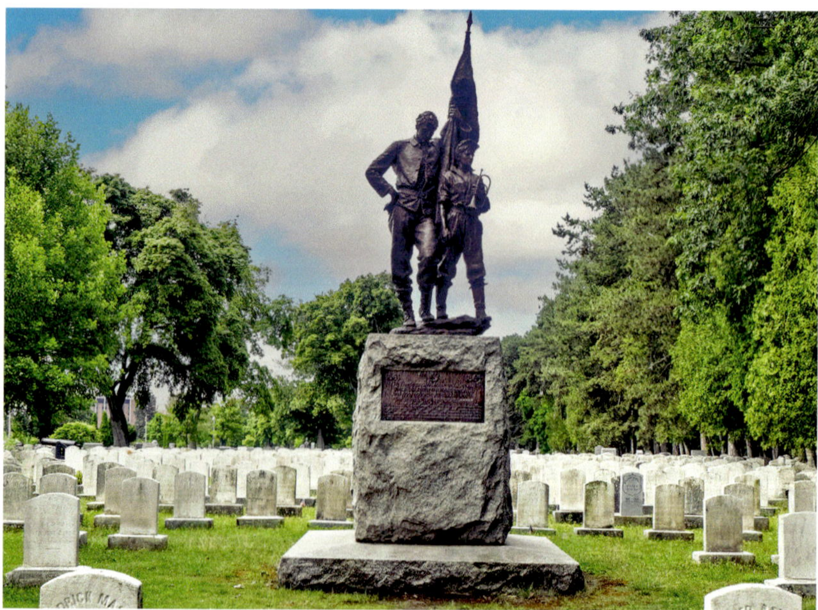

This soldier looks down in grief? exhaustion? despair? He is holding the flag, and by his side a boy holds his bugle. The statue was sculpted by Sally James Farnham in honor of Rochester's Civil War soldiers. A bronze plaque on the base cites a verse from a poem by Theodore Harris: "On Fame's eternal camping ground; Their silent tents are spread; And glory guards with solemn round; The bivouac of the dead."

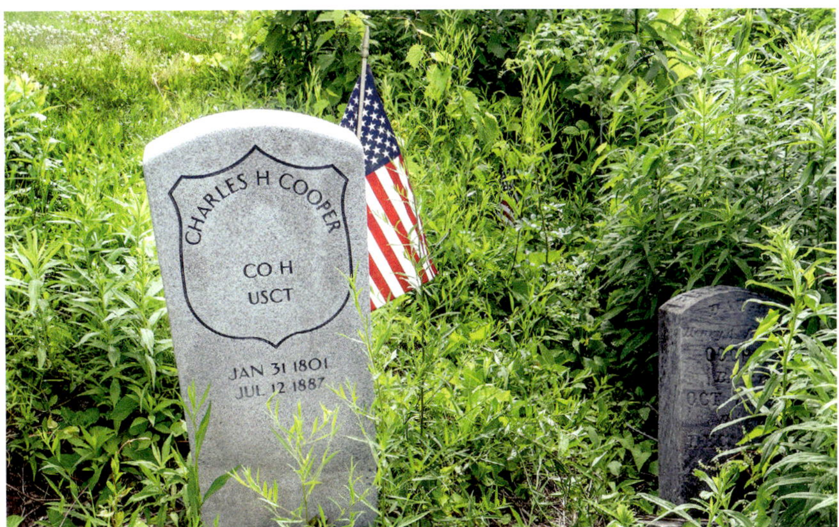

The headstone for Charles Cooper at Bushnell Cemetery, Sodus reads "CO H, USCT" that stands for Company H, United States Colored Troops. During the Civil War, Sgt. Cooper was a member of the 8th Infantry Regiment of African Americans operating out of Philadelphia under the command of Colonel Charles Fribley. The Cooper headstone has historic significance for Sodus. His grandfather, a former slave, was one of the first two African American landowners in the area.

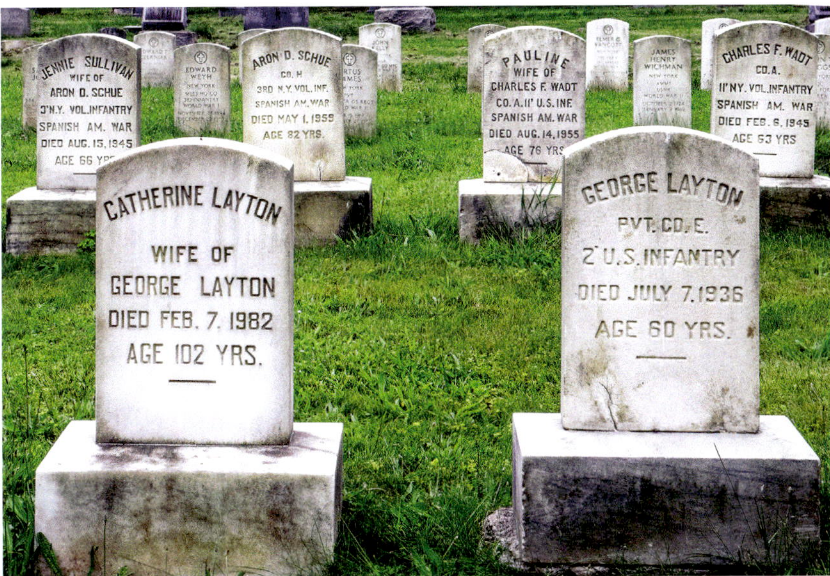

The final war of the century was blessedly short, lasting less than a year. Husband and wife, Catherine and George Layton, are buried together in the Spanish-American War section at Mount Hope Cemetery. He survived the war yet died relatively young. She lived another forty-six years to the ripe old age of 102. Wander through this cemetery, read the stones, and discover remarkable lives represented here.

2
Modern Cemeteries

Cemeteries continued to reflect ongoing change as the twentieth century arrived and progressed. Marble, easily damaged by the elements and prone to breaking, was replaced by granite as the stone of choice. Much harder and more durable than marble, granite is not easy to shape or carve. Headstones became simpler in form.

Garden cemeteries evolved into lawn cemetery designs to accommodate ongoing maintenance, now done by machines. As families became smaller and more dispersed, family plots gave way to individual headstones lined up in rows.

A modification of the lawn cemetery design, the memorial park, gradually became popular. In these areas, headstones were replaced with more uniform plaques flat on the grass. Individual mementos were discouraged to allow for an unimpeded natural setting.

The development of embalming and cremation allowed cost-effective above-ground options in community mausoleums and columbaria. Veterans, whose graves were aligned in military precision, were honored in special locations.

Change continued. As the great wars passed, sandblasting, engraving, and etching allowed more sophisticated designs. A slant-front granite stone—affordable, small, and compact—was developed, allowing each marker to have design features unique for each person.

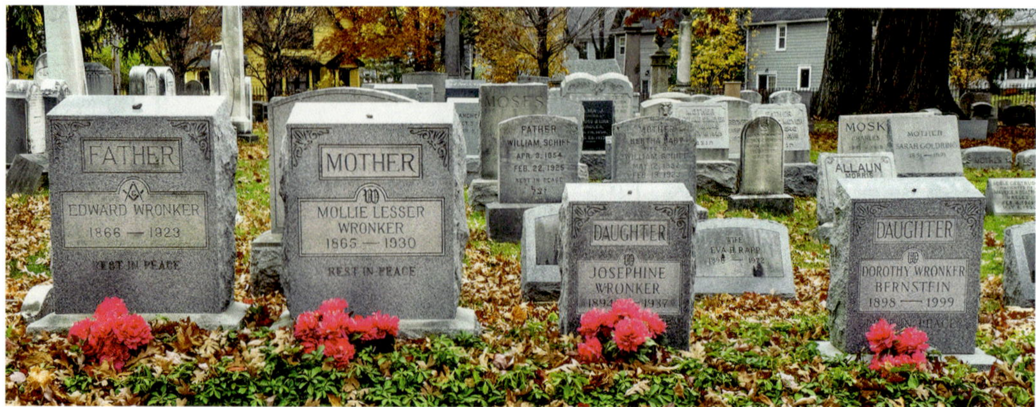

Rectangular granite headstones like these at Mount Hope became the style of choice as the twentieth century emerged.

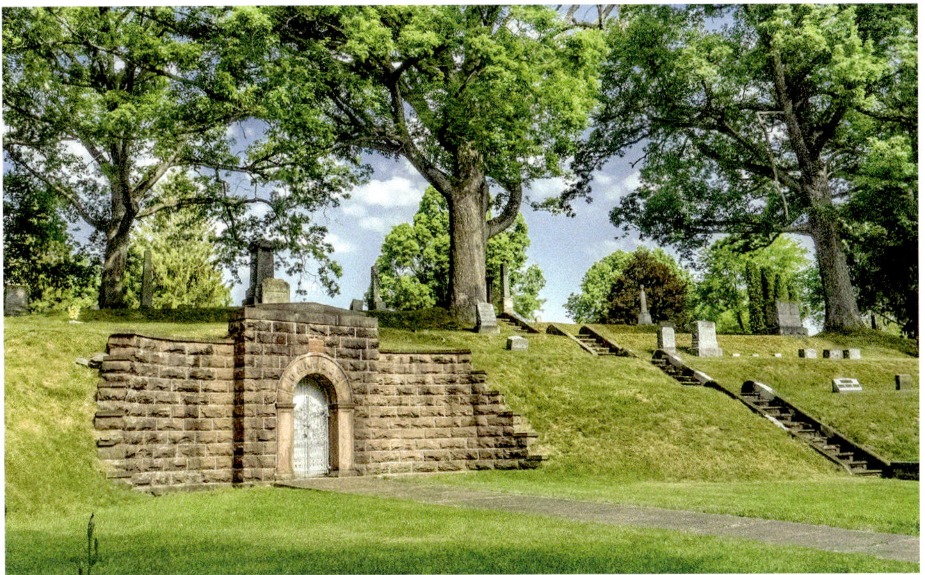

In the days of hand-dug graves, places were needed to store the deceased when the ground was frozen. These "receiving vaults" often were dug into a hillside to take advantage of natural insulation. Nunda Cemetery was long established when a receiving vault and stairway were added during the early 1900s.

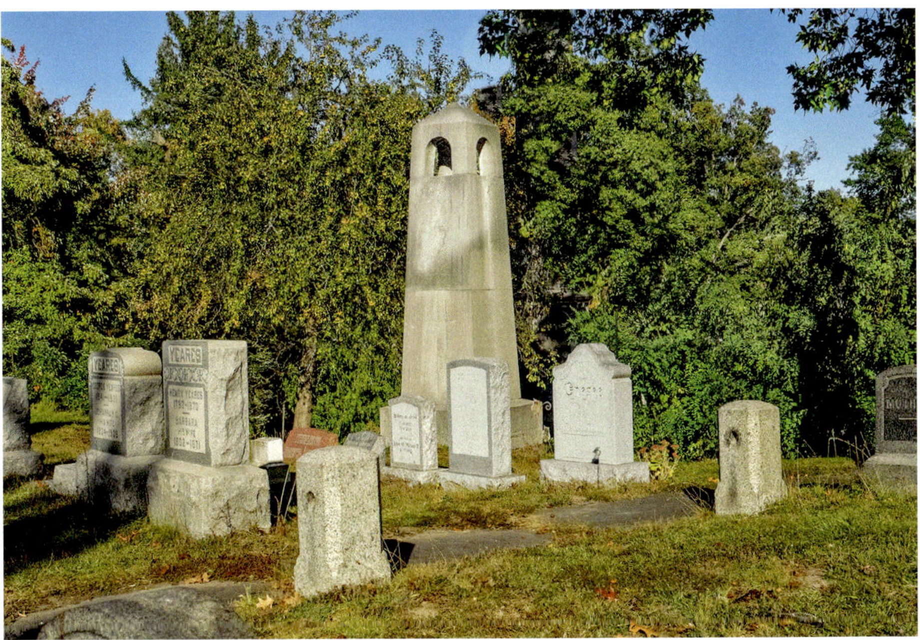

Receiving vaults need a ventilation system. This handsome obelisk like "monument" at Mount Hope is a cleverly designed ventilation stack from the receiving vault attached to the Old Chapel at the base of the hillside below. It blends nicely with surrounding markers.

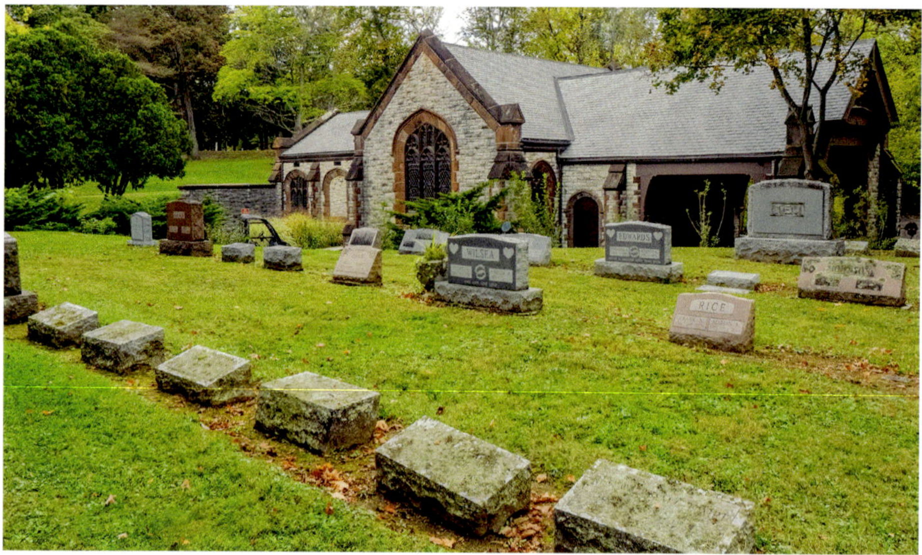

Many garden cemeteries created chapels for services and events at the cemetery. Canandaigua's Woodlawn Cemetery erected theirs in 1909 through the generosity of Mary Clark Thompson. Designed by architect Francis R. Allen, it was constructed from local limestone trimmed with Medina sandstone. The stained-glass windows in the chapel were imported from England. The chapel has been thoughtfully reconstructed and again is in use.

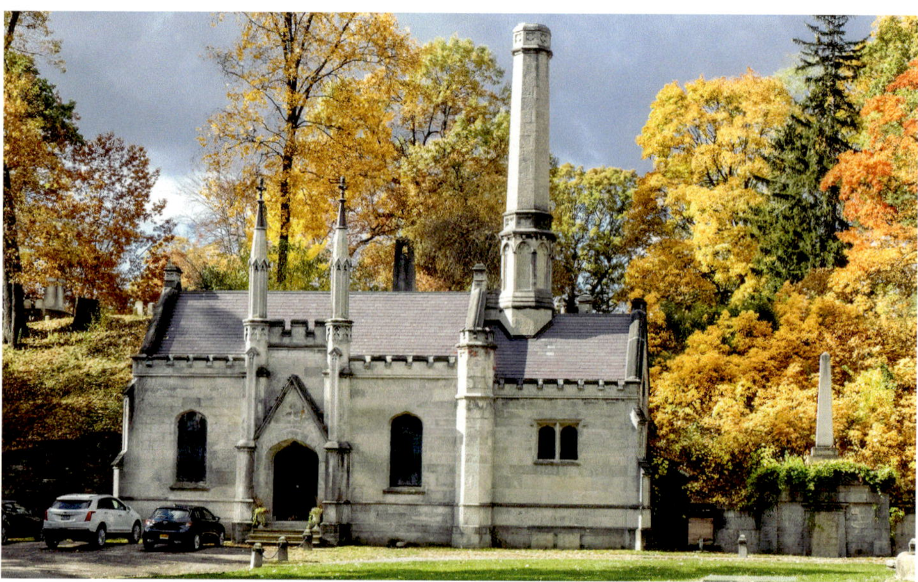

At about the same time, cremation became available in this area. Mount Hope added a crematory constructed as an aesthetic addition (note tall chimney) to the original 1862 chapel and receiving vault. Architect Foster Warner carefully planned the addition that housed two massive ovens. The ovens, called retorts, provided heat from below, allowing the ashes of the deceased to be isolated and recovered for the family.

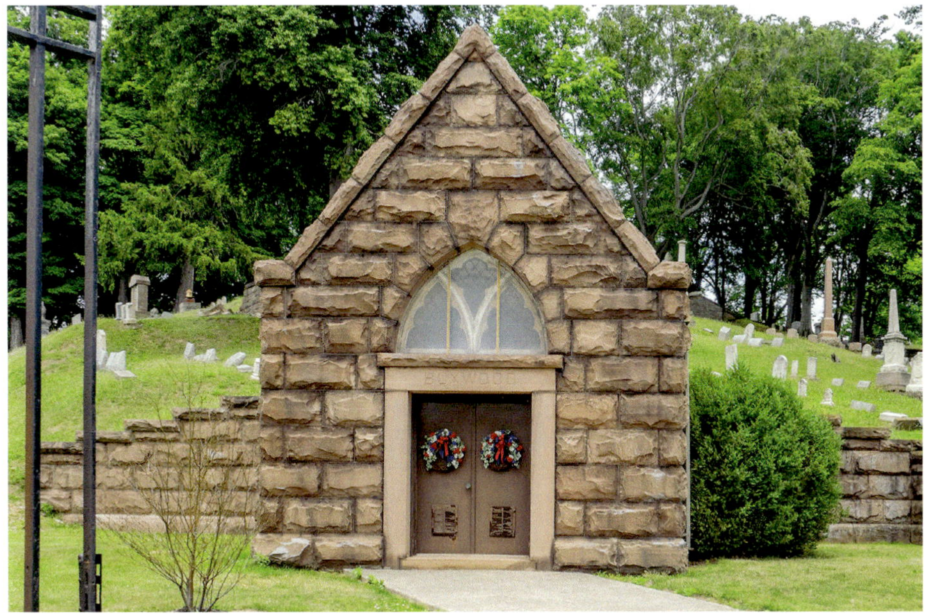

The Burroughs Chapel was constructed of Medina sandstone at Boxwood Cemetery, Medina in 1903. As too often has occurred, this chapel fell into disrepair. In 2024, the Friends of Boxwood Cemetery celebrated its restoration. I had the opportunity to watch as Valerie O'Hara of Pike Stained Glass worked to restore the lovely stained-glass window to its original condition. The window remains a fitting memorial to the donor of the refurbished chapel and receiving vault that grace the south entrance to the cemetery.

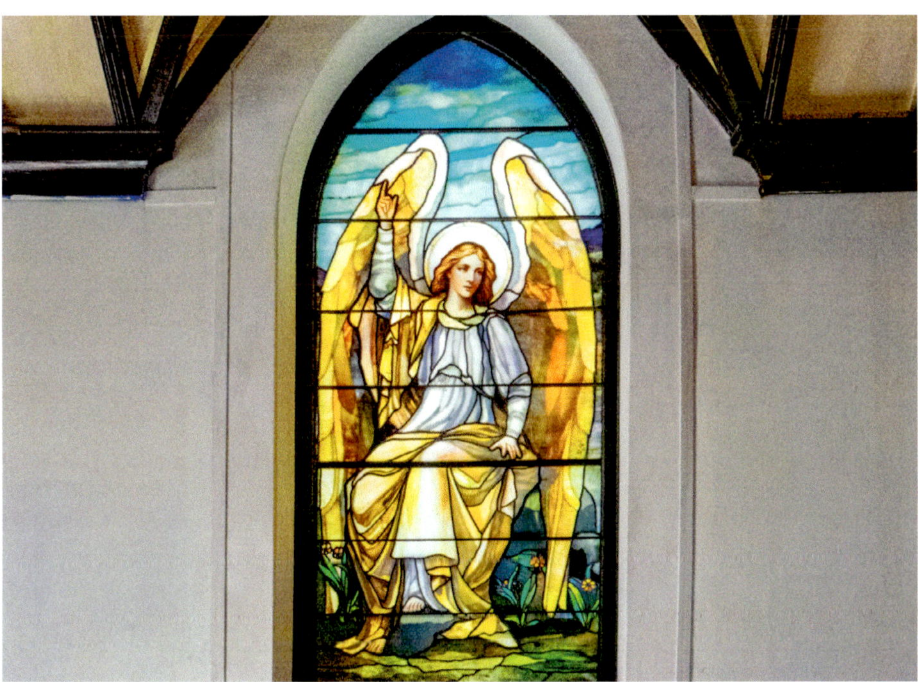

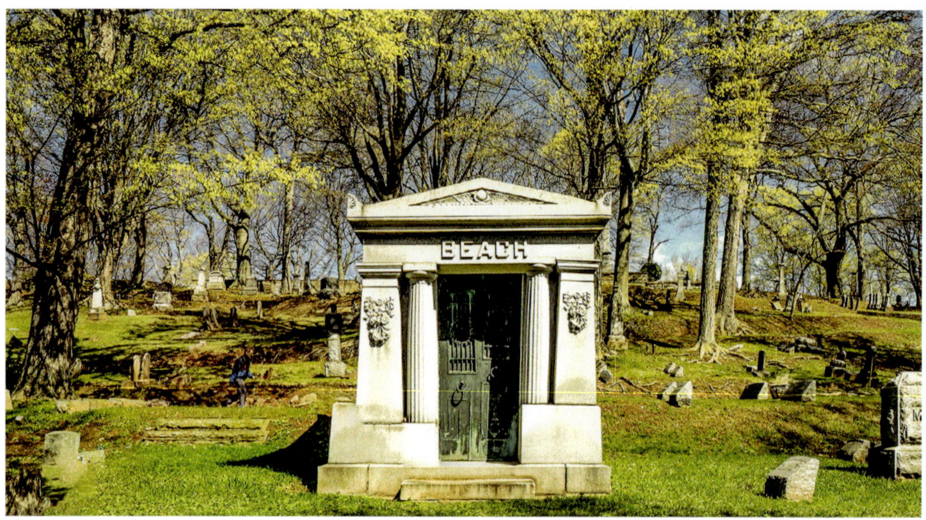

Above-ground interment was a new option for family mausoleums after the Civil War, when embalming became more widespread. The Myra and Frank Beach mausoleum erected at Boxwood Cemetery in 1902 sits at the foot of a hill amidst trees that seem like giants towering behind the structure. Constructed of rough and smooth granite, it combines neoclassical and Egyptian-revival features.

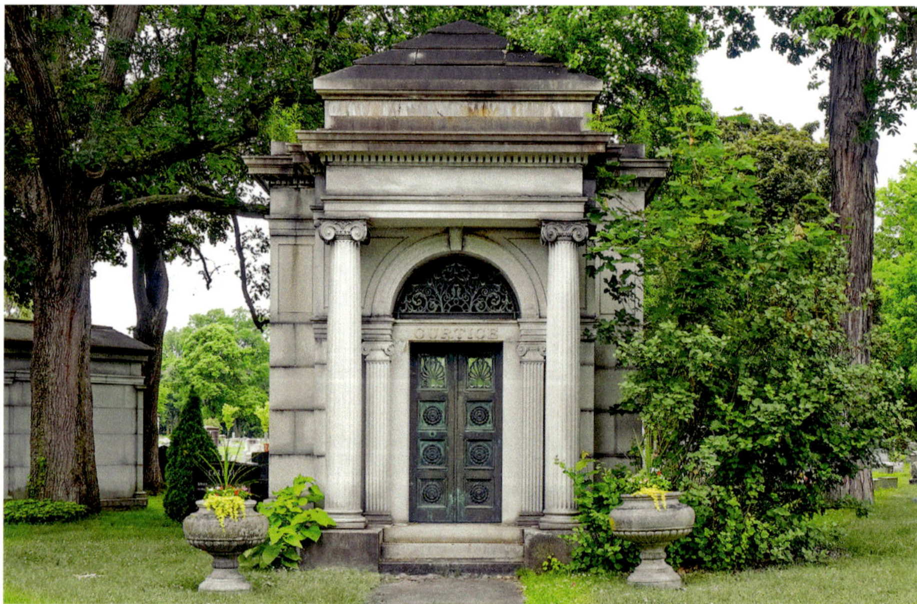

While exploring the Christina and Simeon Goodnow Curtice mausoleum at Mount Hope, I realized that Simeon is the grandson of the Goodnows buried in Webster Union Cemetery (pictured early in the previous chapter). The cemetery serves as a history book: grandsons Simeon and Edgar Curtice developed a very successful canning business with our abundant local produce. In the early 1900s, Curtice Brothers Blue Label Ketchup rivaled Heinz in popularity.

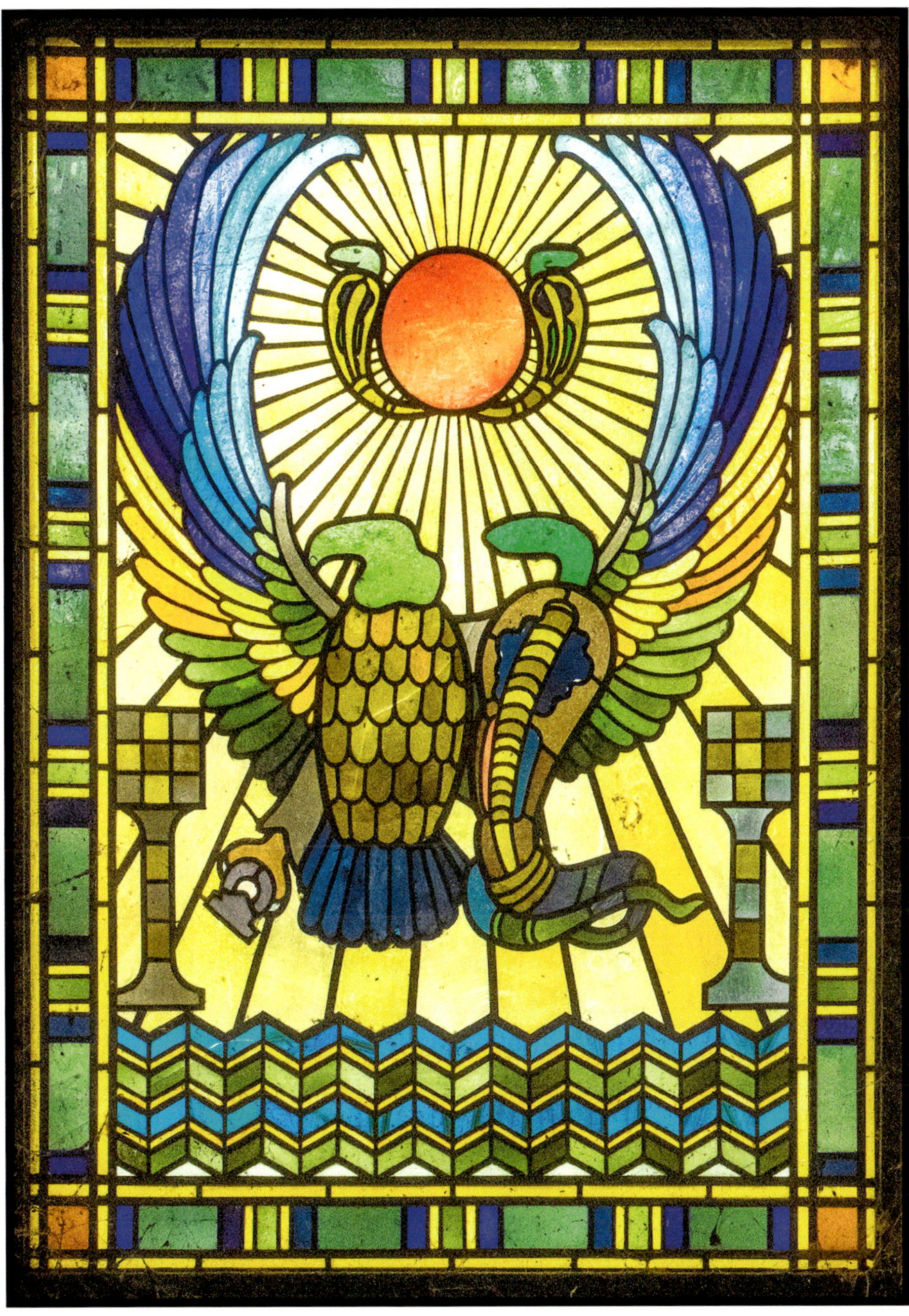

Riverside Cemetery in Rochester has a handsome tomb for Julia and John Kent and their daughter, Ada. Stained-glass windows often graced mausoleums of this period. In this tomb, an extraordinary window shows a serpent representing royalty and divinity, an eagle standing for strength, courage, and wisdom, and the goddess Nekhbet as the protector of the pharaoh.

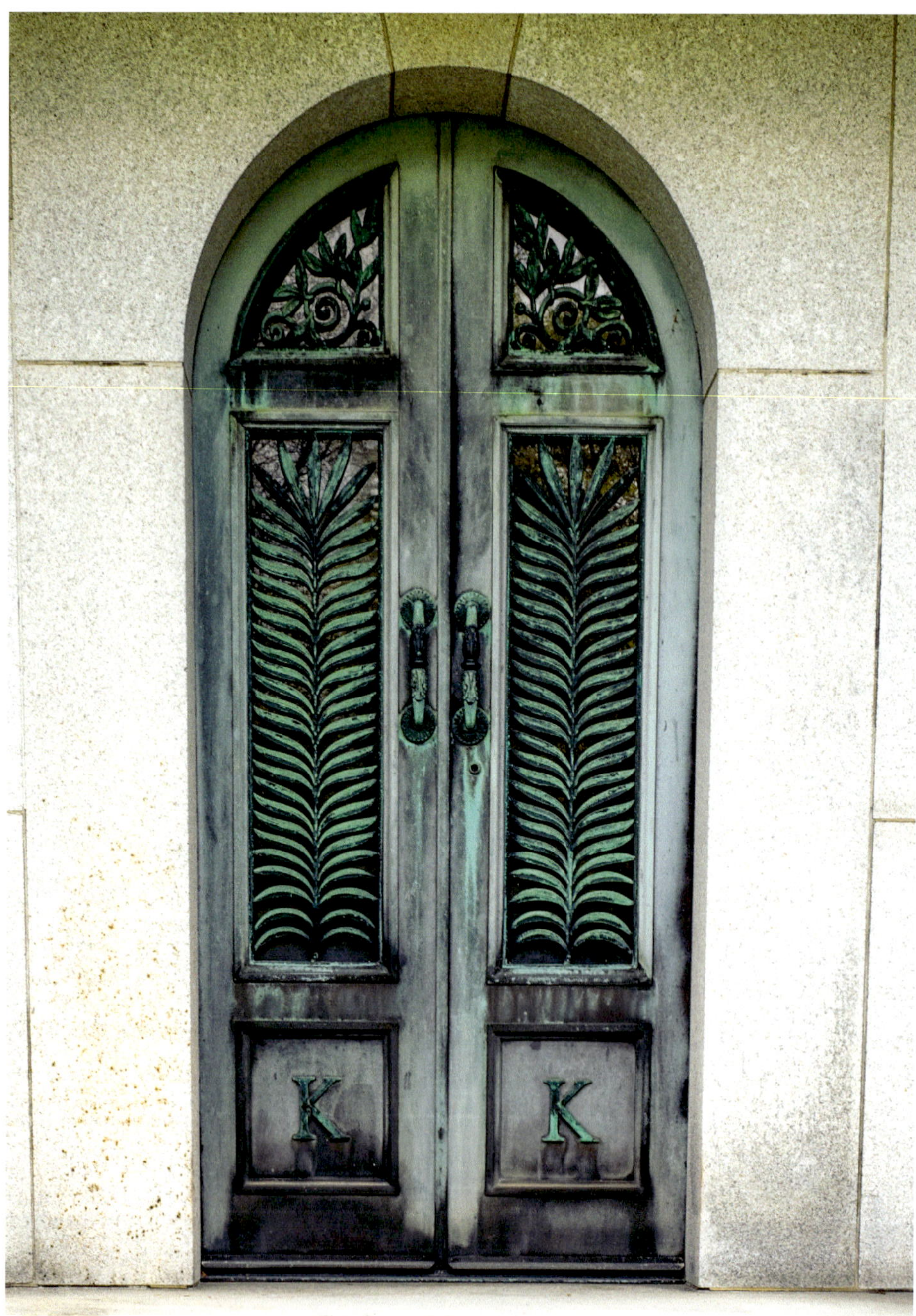

Many family mausolea have intriguing doors designed both for protection and to make visible the crypts and stained-glass window inside. The oval-shaped door of the Elizabeth and William Kelly mausoleum at Cold Springs Cemetery, Lockport is constructed with a repetitive palm frond pattern adding elegance to the simplicity of the building structure.

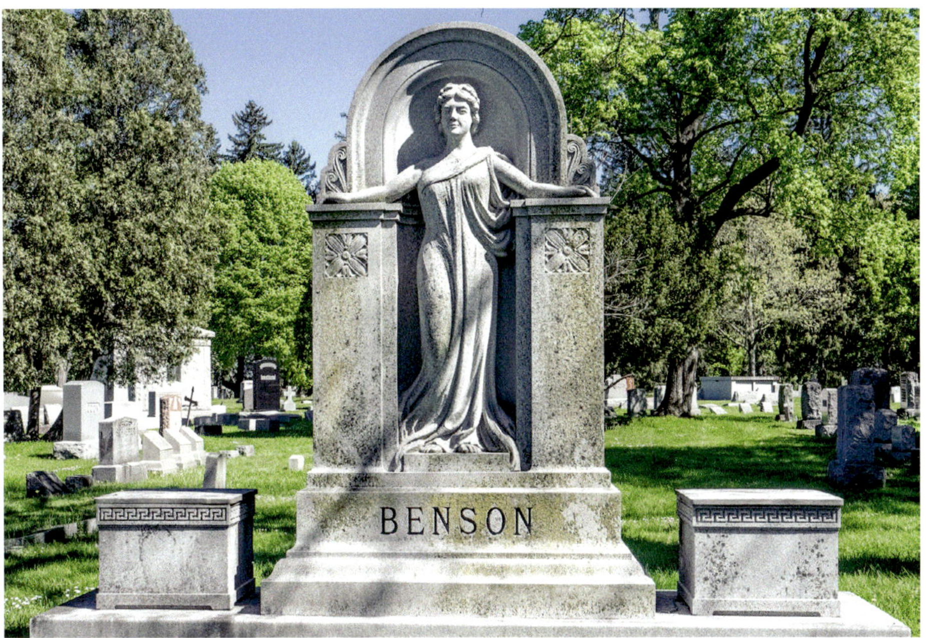

Mount Hope Cemetery is an excellent place to see stylistic transitions from the nineteenth into the twentieth centuries. The monument for Sofia and John Benson melds a classical look from the past with twentieth-century simplicity, incorporating new materials and stone carving techniques.

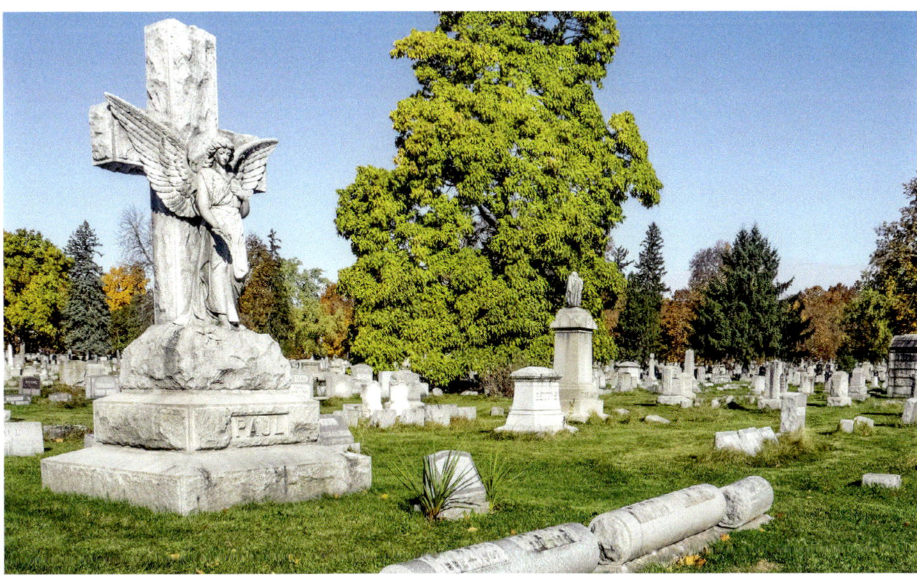

As the century moved on, many Victorian styles took on more modern forms. The Paul family angel in Mount Hope range 4 is created in rough stone with a very solid appearance. Compare this to the nineteenth-century Likly family angel near the Copper Beach in section L.

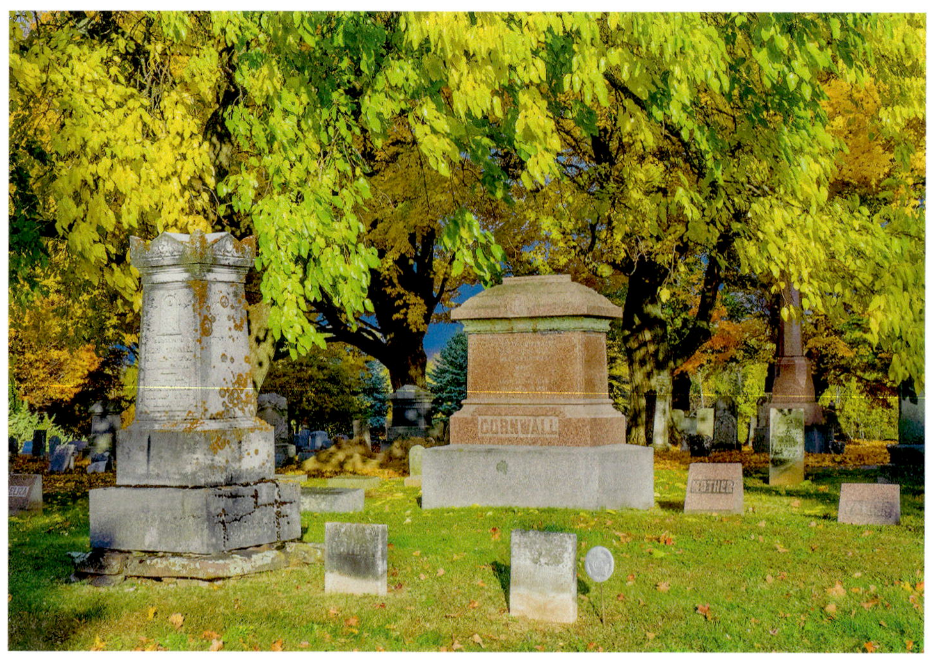

Many of our local cemeteries have a wonderful mix of Victorian and modern, marble and granite, classic and simpler contemporary styles. At Lakeview Cemetery, Pultneyville (above), an older marble monument in truncated classic style is next to a massive highly polished granite stone capped with a "roof" marking a family plot. Lakeview Cemetery in Penn Yan (below) has a marker combining unfinished sections with a polished face. Varying examples of this style can be seen in many of the area cemeteries.

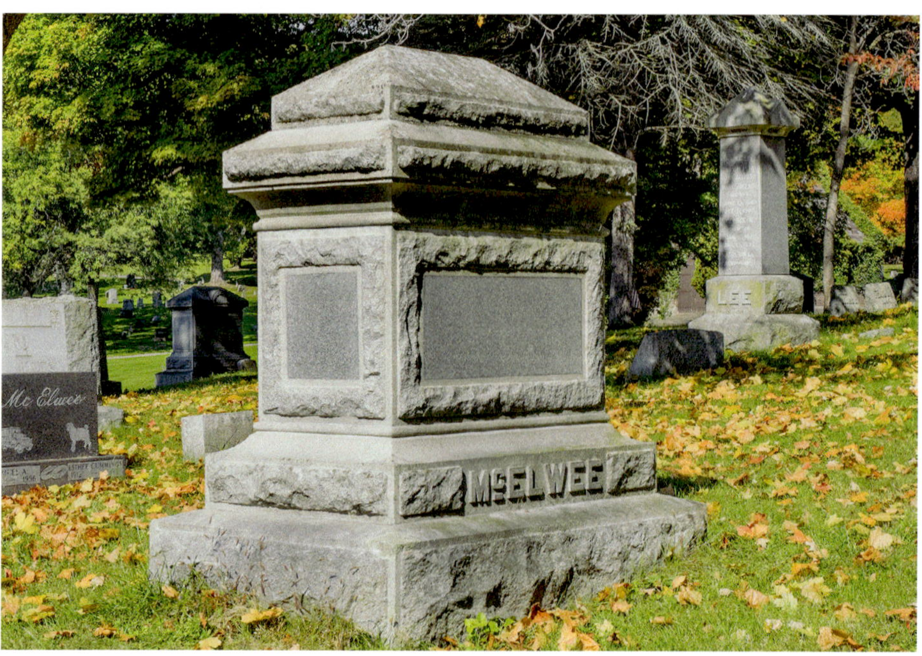

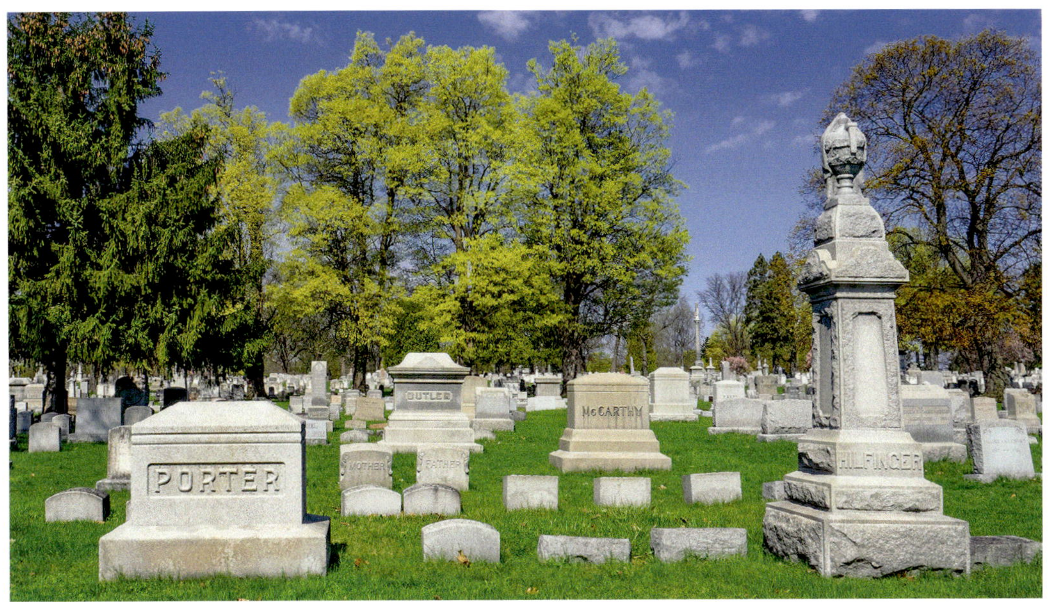

Garden cemeteries like Mount Hope, Boxwood, and Mount Albion faced overwhelming maintenance issues as time went by. Caring for picturesque family plots on hilly terrain was difficult. As family sizes decreased and children moved to new areas, smaller plots became popular. Flat sections were converted to even rows of individual markers allowing easier maintenance with the recently developed lawn mower. Mount Hope (above) and Britton Road Cemetery (below) show the transition of styles as the twentieth century progressed towards rows of headstones with simple clean lines.

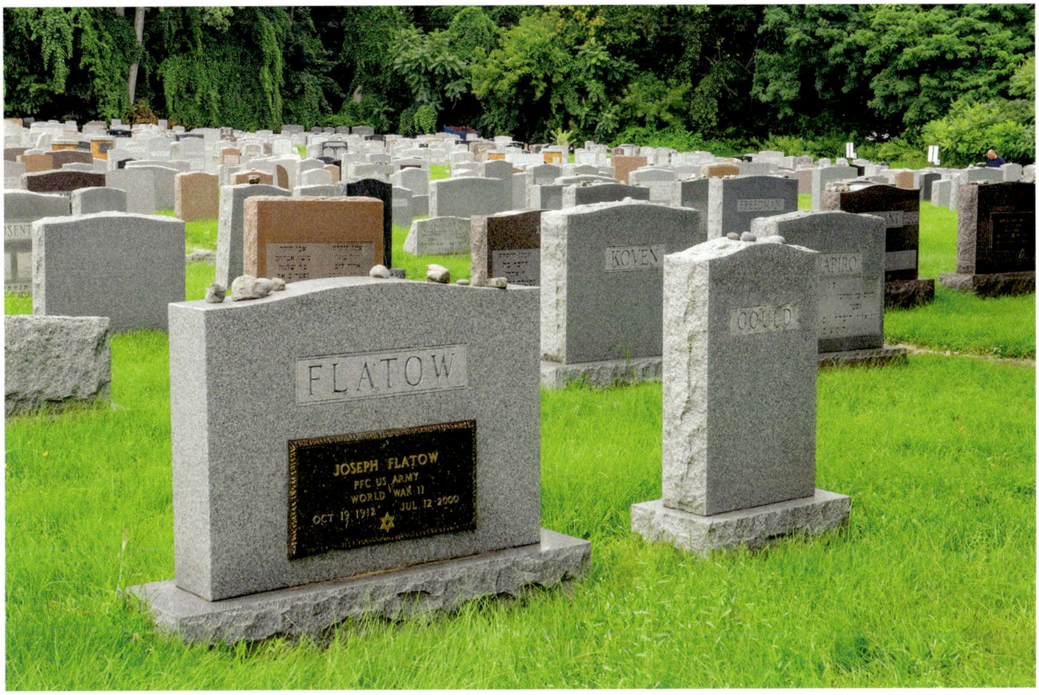

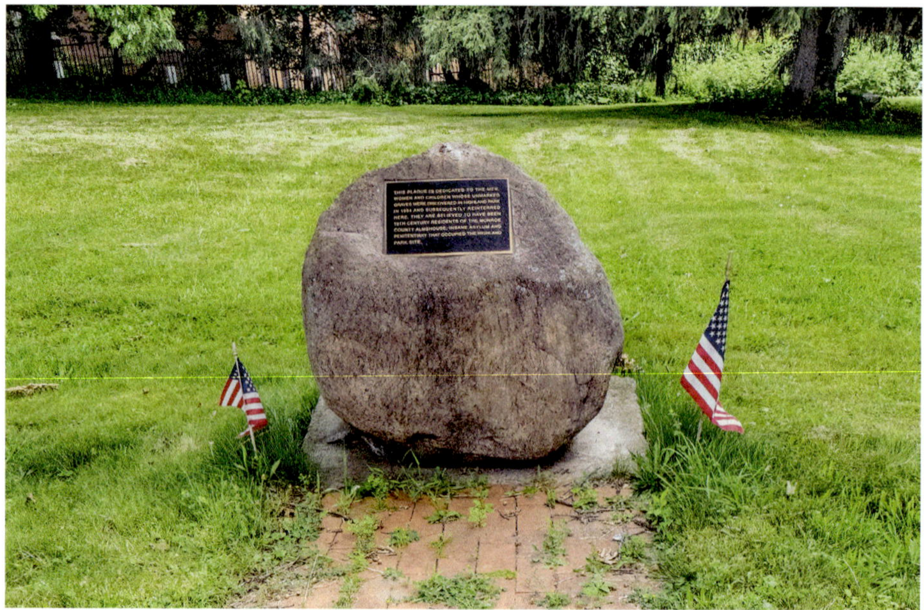

In a modern throwback to the early settlers' use of field stone markers, large natural stone boulders left by the glaciers have been used as monuments. Here at Mount Hope a plaque has been added honoring the reburial of residents of the nineteenth century almshouse, asylum and penitentiary buildings originally on the site of Highland Park. Striking markers like this also have been used for family plots in Honeoye Falls and Seneca Falls.

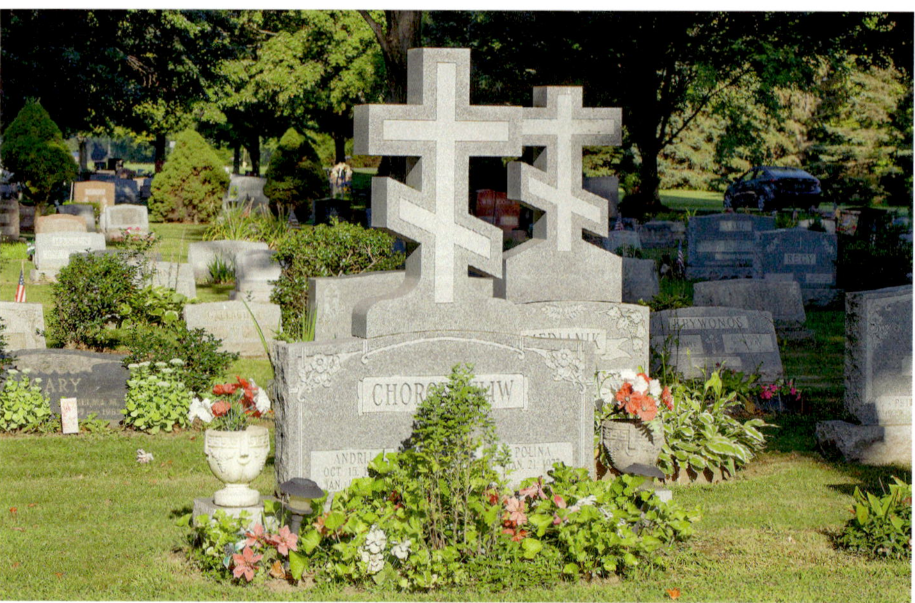

Another distinctive modern adaptation of traditional grave markers can be seen at Webster Union Cemetery, where this pair of crosses shines in the morning light.

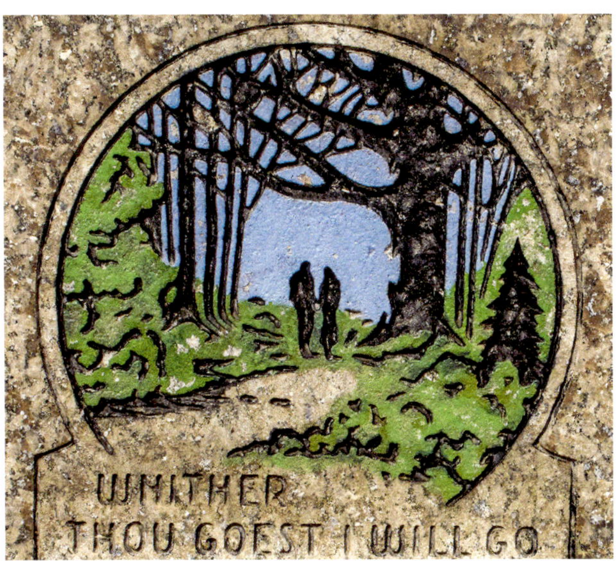

After visiting several area cemeteries, certain types and styles of monuments begin to look familiar. It is a surprise, however, to find identical motifs such as these 30 miles apart. I found the first (above) in Webster Union Cemetery in 2014. Then I happened upon the very same design at Boughton Hill Cemetery ten years later. In the early part of the century, similar monuments could be ordered through the Sears catalog. Today they can be ordered online. While it might not be surprising to see the same design in two different cemeteries, this design particularly stands out because it employs color.

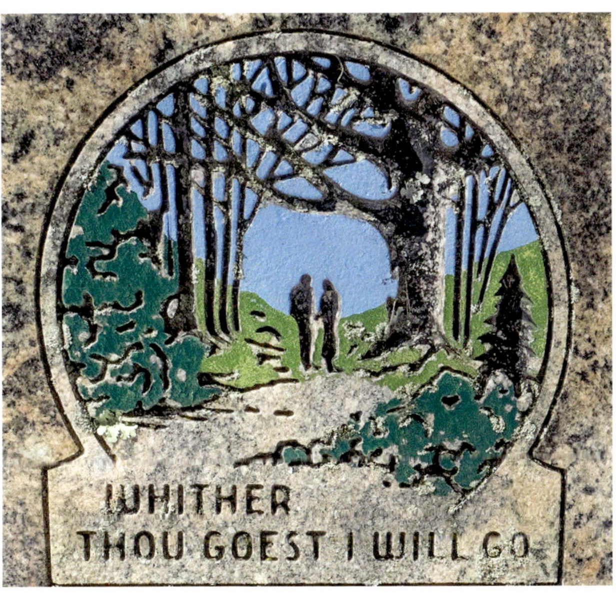

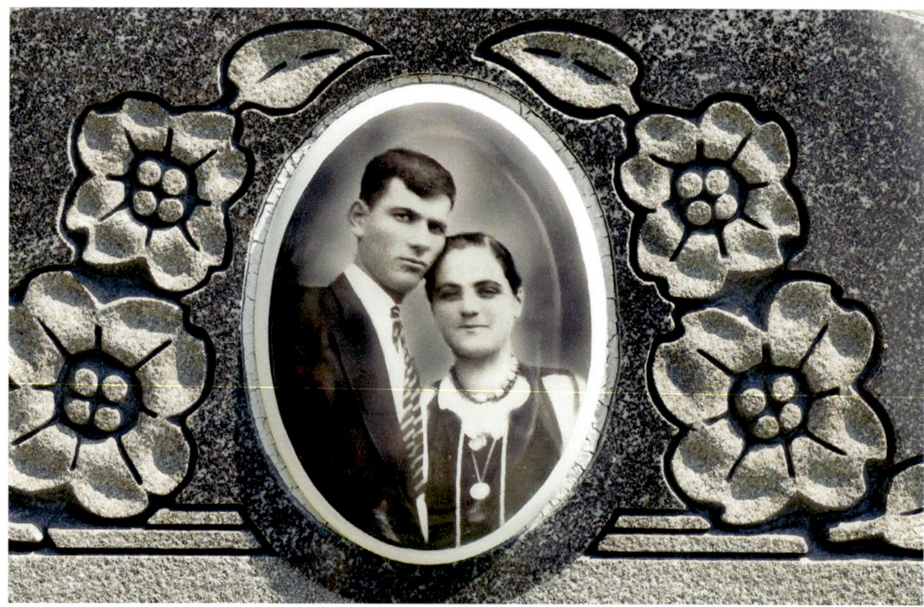

The new century brought immigrants with their own cemetery traditions. One was the placement of a ceramic photo on the headstone. Two headstones at Mount Hope show the range of ceramic photo design in the twentieth century. The marker for Kalina and Soter (above) from early in the century features a prominent ceramic oval surrounded by a deeply etched flower design. The headstone below honors a large family group, with burials extending into the twenty-first century. The images are smaller to accommodate twelve members of the Ferris family. Today the process involves attaching an image to a decal, which then is fired onto a ceramic blank in a kiln. Like so many other products, these now can be ordered online.

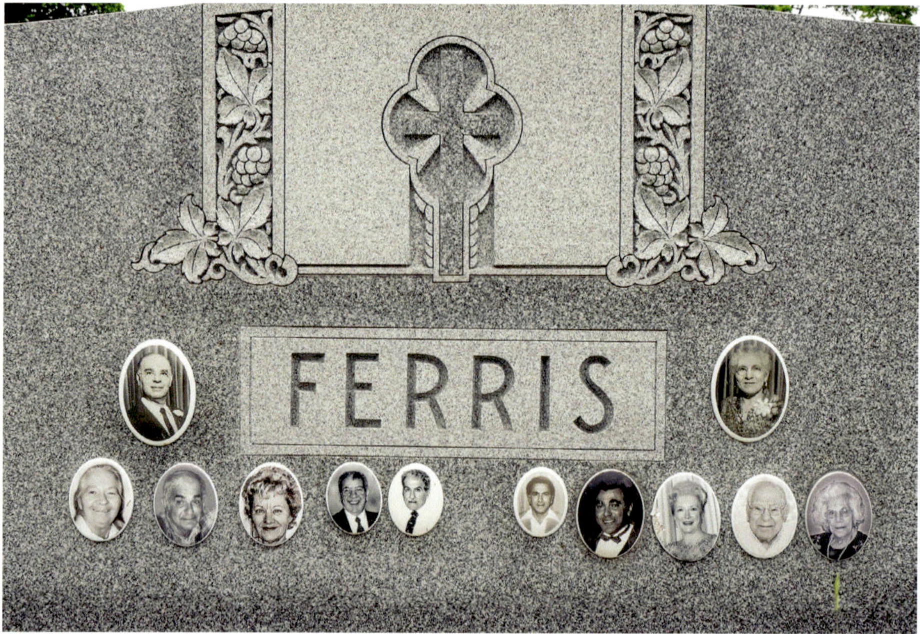

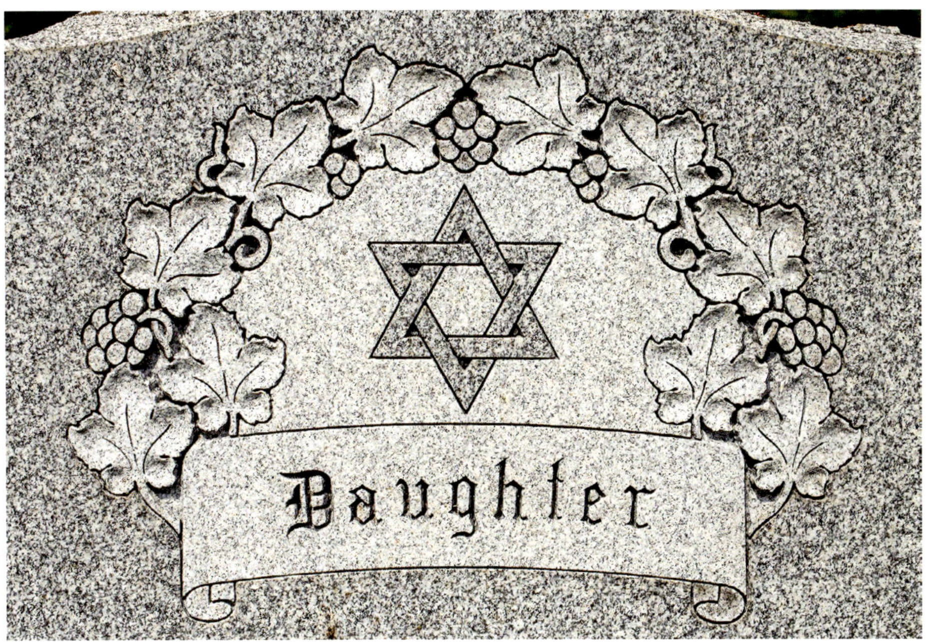

Designs personalize a stone. Marble is relatively soft, easily carved with traditional tools. Granite requires something stronger. Sandblasting and engraving can give depth and detail to a design. On this monument the leaves and berries are deeply etched, surrounding the Jewish star cut into a polished face, with the word daughter underneath.

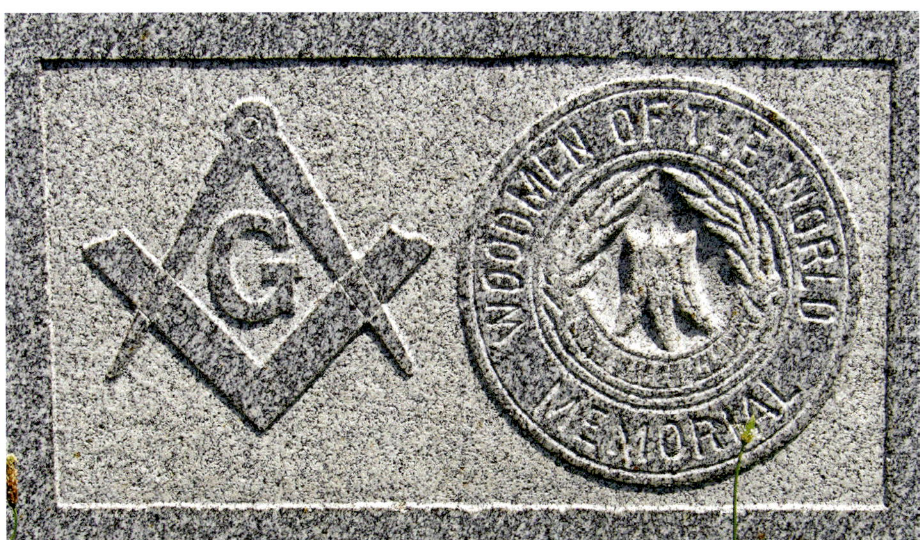

Symbols of association membership have been a source of personalization throughout the twentieth century. This marker at Mount Hope features symbols of the Masonic and Woodmen of the World associations. Rather than being carved into the stone, this design has been created by removing portions of the stone around the design.

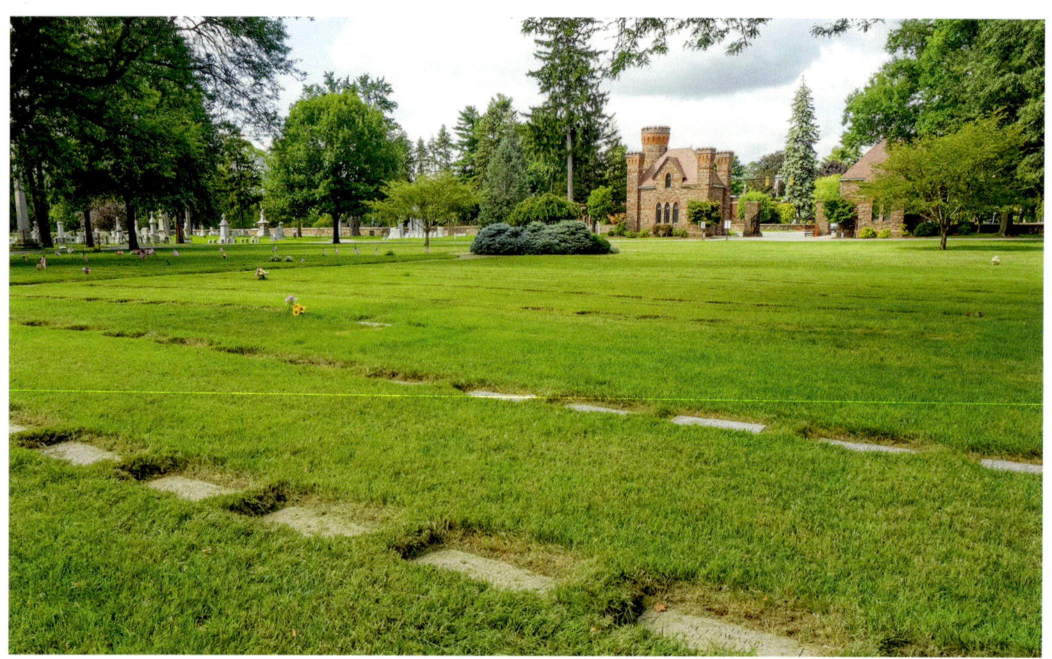

Memorial park cemetery design in the Rochester area features plaques placed flat on the grass with minimal adornment. Irondequoit and Holy Sepulchre have designated areas for this type of burial. Holy Sepulchre (above) also features plaque memorials for Catholic sisters. A daffodil blooms at each marker in the spring. Whitehaven Memorial Park, Pittsford (below), combines the traditional Victorian garden cemetery concept with a modern-day memorial garden. In this case, the grand monuments are the impressive trees, while the plaques, uniform in size and shape, lie unobtrusively on the ground. Whitehaven is a designated Audubon and Arboretum area with a hiking trail at the rear.

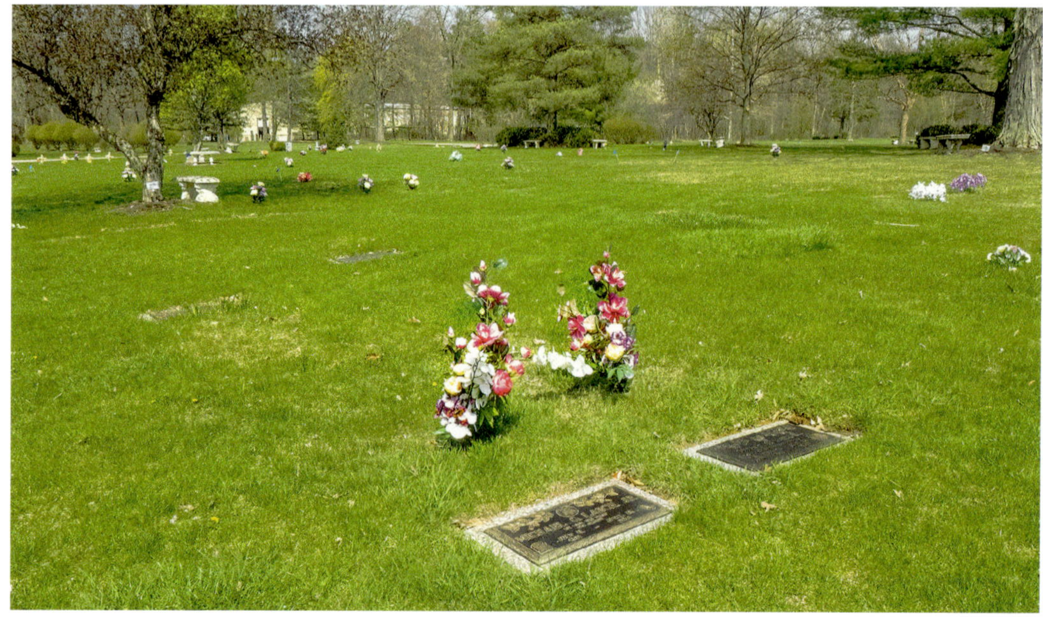

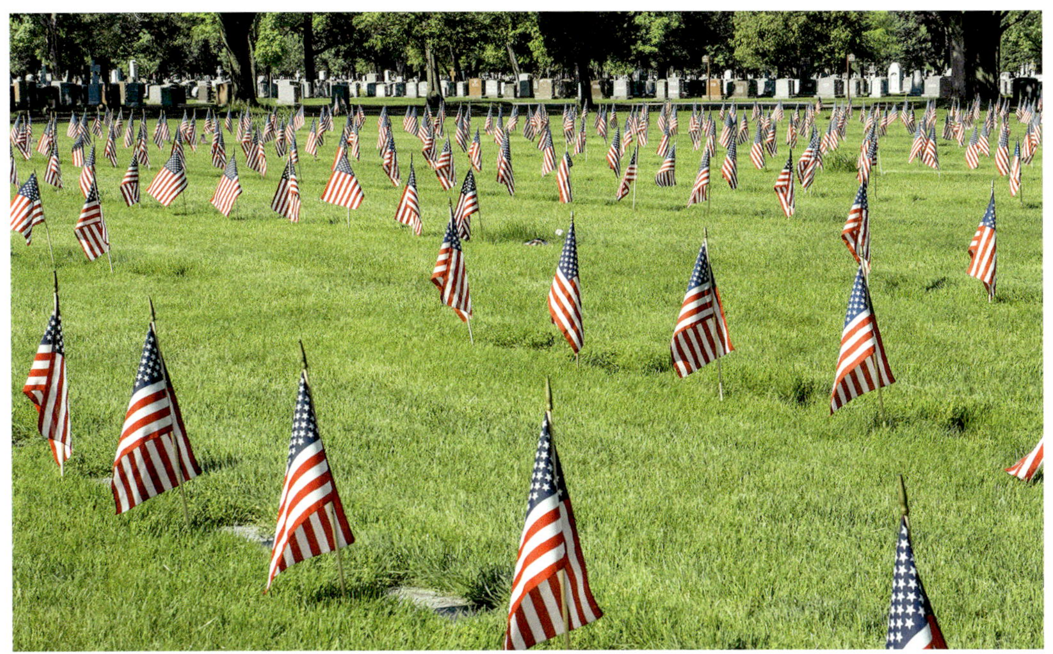

Memorial park design also can be found in special areas set aside for veterans. This section at Holy Sepulchre Cemetery (above) is quite moving at holiday time. Other cemeteries use a traditional federal, rounded top, marble-style marker. Still others use designs unique to their cemetery. Mount Albion (below) has experimented with varying marker styles in different sections, and burials include spouses. Smaller cemeteries honor their veterans with bronze plaques on the rear of the headstone, and some celebrate with Wreaths Across America at winter holiday time.

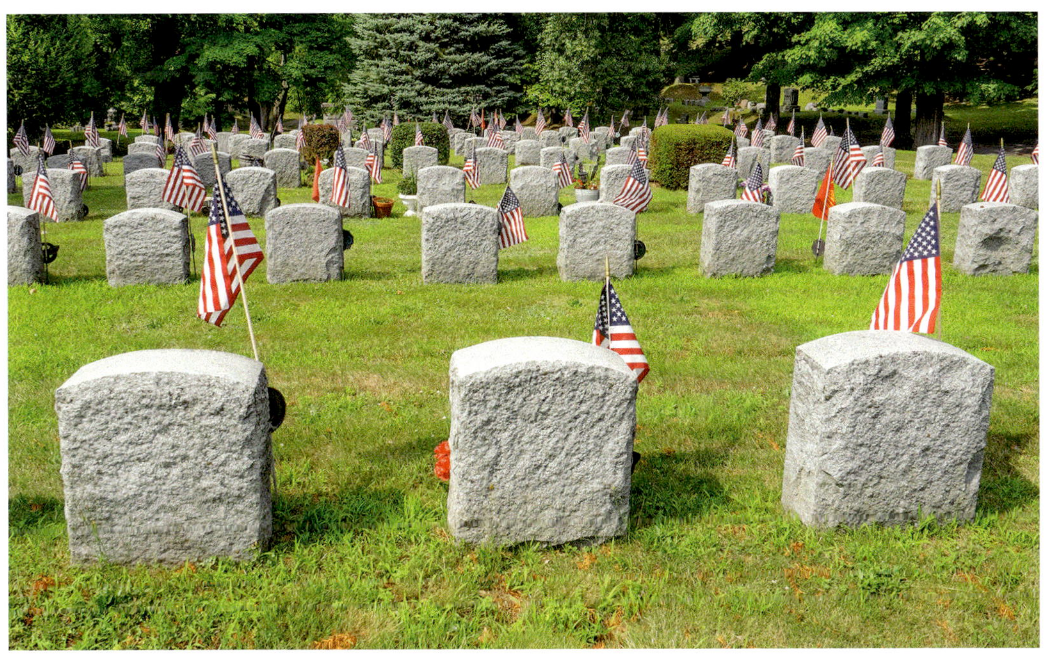

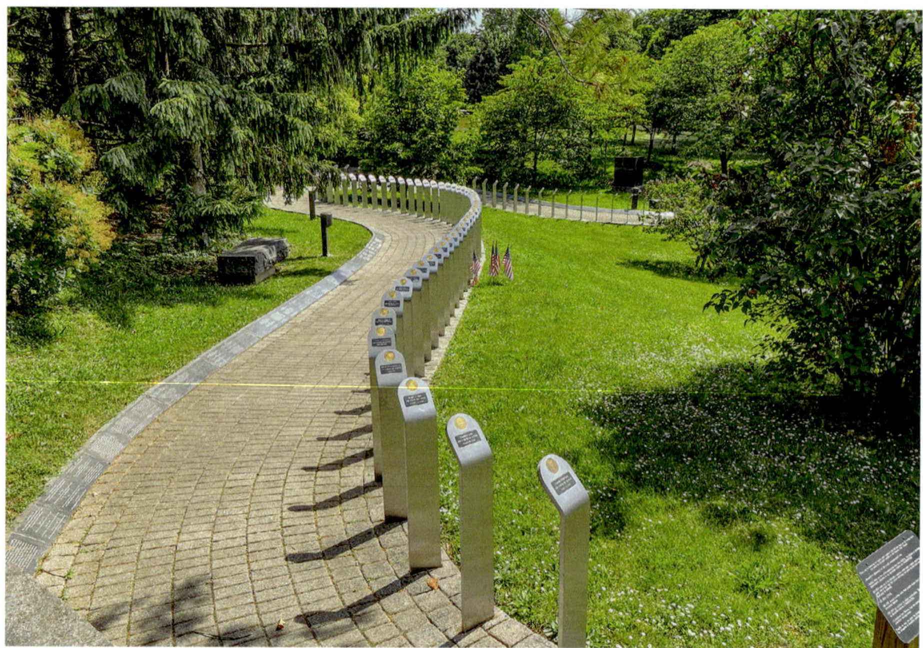

I was deeply moved by the Vietnam Memorial in Rochester, which presents not just the heroism but also the toll of war on both those who died and those who live on with their injuries. Opposite the bollards that represent each local person who died is a line of flat plaques well worth reading. They detail the escalation and ending of the war.

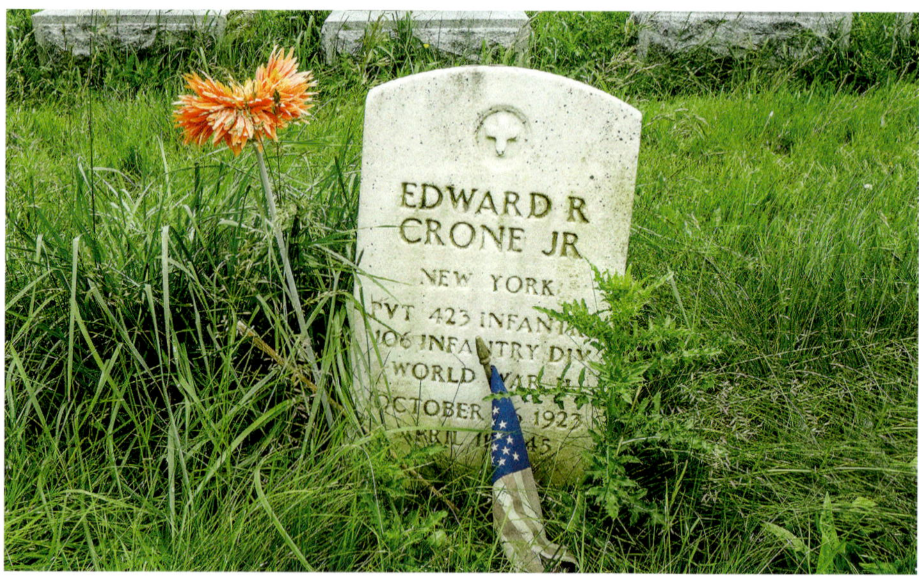

A small, isolated stone at Mount Hope for Edward Crone is another example of the tragedy of war. The memorial honors the man who was the inspiration for the character Billy Pilgrim in Kurt Vonnegut's *Slaughterhouse 5*.

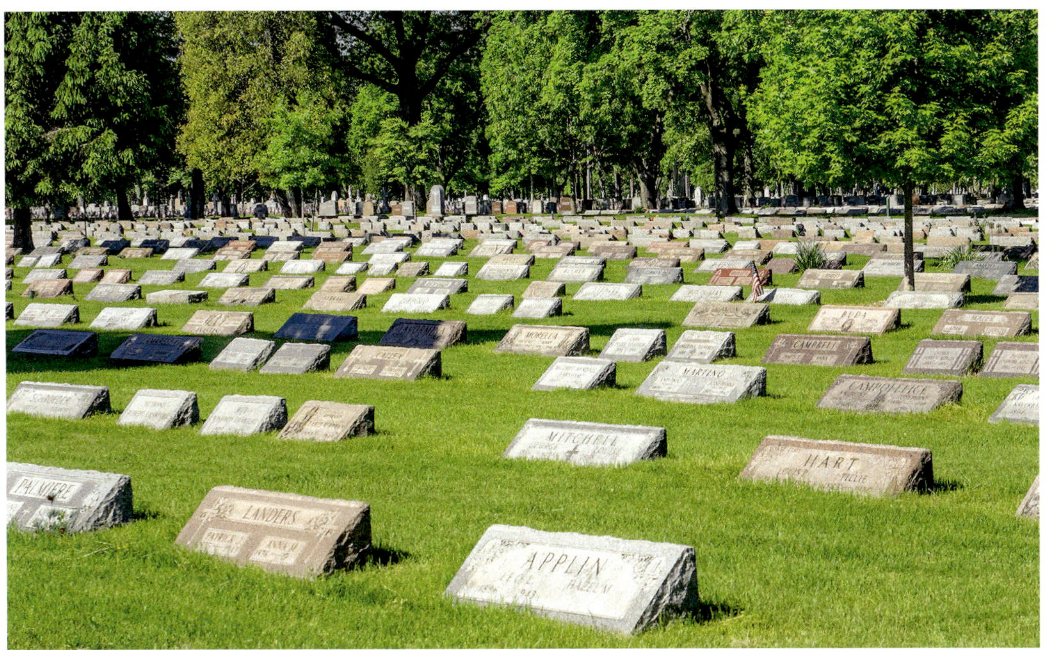

The ubiquitous slant-front monument is a fitting way to end this chapter. Popular because it is affordable and can be tailored to each family's specifications, the polished slant front has enough space for names, dates, and a personalized design. This section at Holy Sepulchre (above) is reminiscent of the military precision of veterans' areas. Do not discount these areas as being all the same though. Each stone has a unique story to tell. Below, the stones at Webster Rural mix well with rectangular markers, shining in the early morning light.

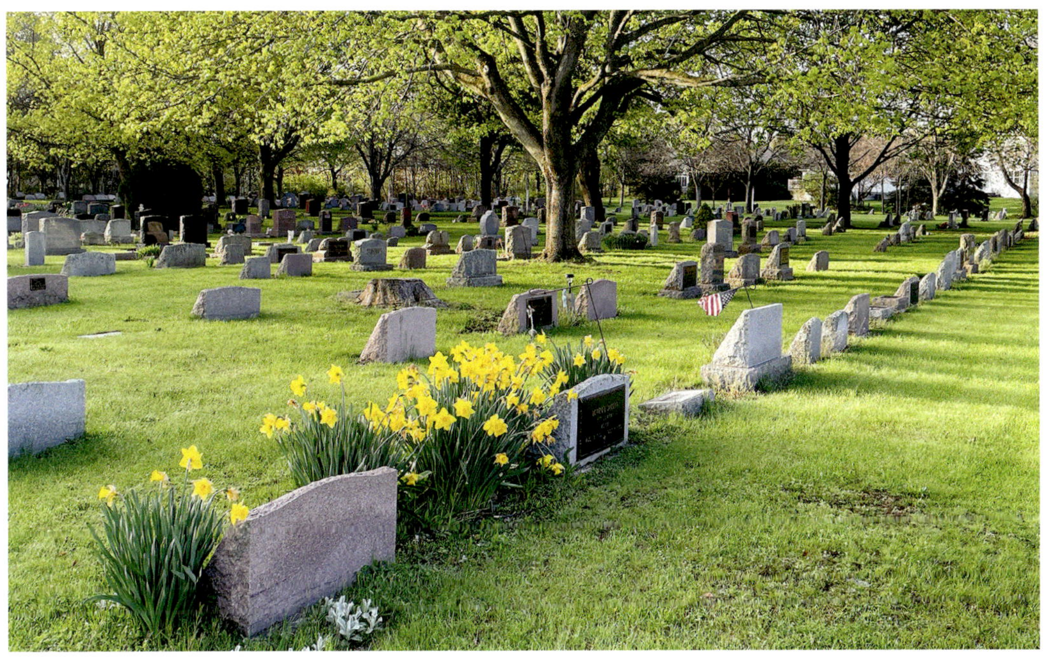

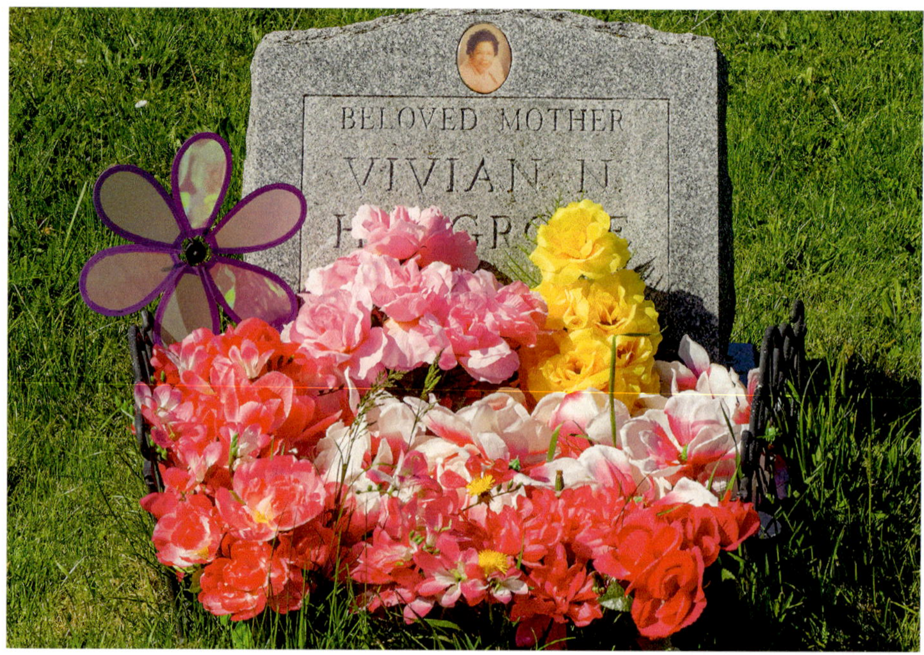

Flowers have been present in cemeteries as far back as 62,000 BCE. They lend an air of comfort at the grave. They are equally poignant gracing a freshly dug grave, with a small stone like this one, or as part of a grand bouquet.

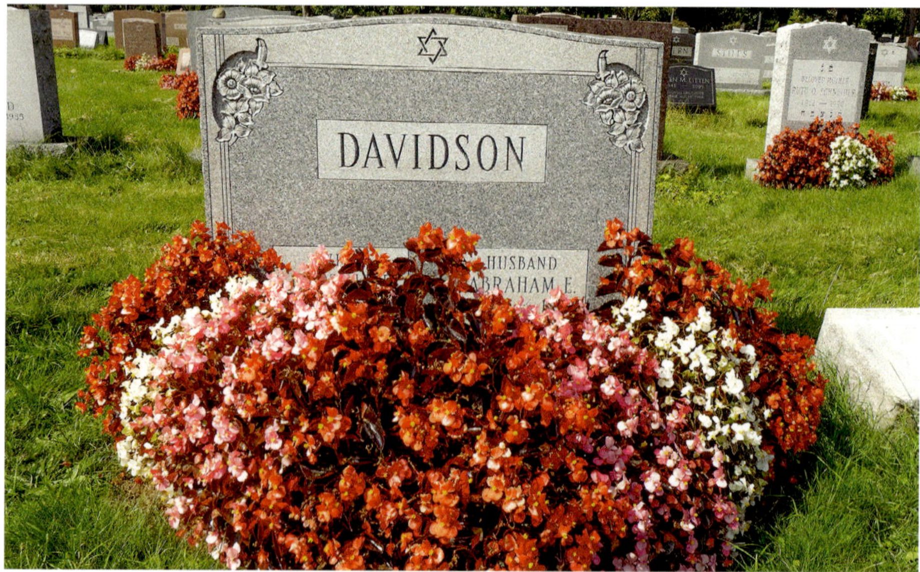

Many cemeteries allow plantings at the gravesite. Caring for a gravesite extends the care that we are no longer able to give to someone who is gone. It provides an excuse to visit, to putter, and perhaps to have a "conversation" at the same time. Returning frequently to a grave can help in the painful process of saying goodbye.

3
Contemporary Cemeteries

The twenty-first century is here. Most Rochester area cemeteries have enough space to continue accommodating new burials. Older generations are commingled with the new, strengthening the sense of history that is so important for a town's identity.

Since the pandemic, death is talked about more openly. More people seem to feel at ease walking through a cemetery, savoring its peace and quiet while visiting loved ones. People picnic at Mount Hope, look for deer at Holy Sepulchre, celebrate town historic events, and volunteer with like-minded people in small and large burial grounds.

Rarely can you find new grand statues such as those in an older garden cemetery. Yet developments in stone-cutting techniques allow exquisite shaping of new monuments for those with deeper pockets. Ceramic photographs continue to add a personal touch. Sophisticated laser designs copied from photographs expand headstone options. Community mausoleums and columbaria are now included in many cemeteries to accommodate those choosing above ground options and cremation, an increasingly popular choice.

Cemeteries are a powerful setting for remembrance and solace. Families gather at the gravesite on anniversaries and holidays. Often mementos may be left at the site to personalize the space.

Traditional memorials and services are sure to continue. But complementing them are new options for cremated remains and green burials. Many funerals no longer are held in churches. Rather, they have become celebratory events at funeral homes, a park, or family gathering place. Often, they can be streamed online for distant friends and family. People are memorialized on Facebook. It will be intriguing to discover just what further changes the future brings.

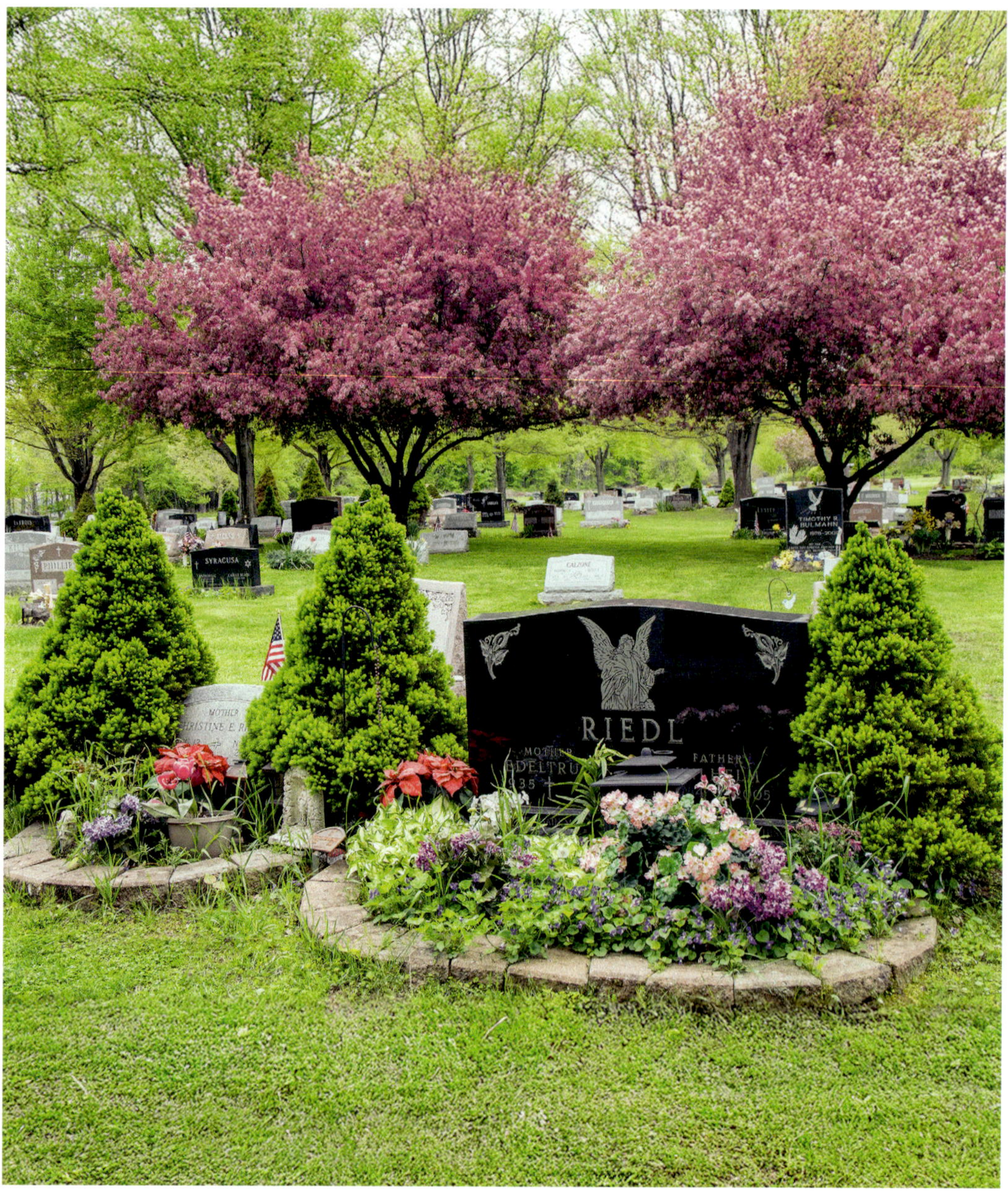

Individual headstones continue to dominate most local cemeteries. Enriched by personal touches and attractive plantings, they are nestled among mature trees and become part of the landscape of time.

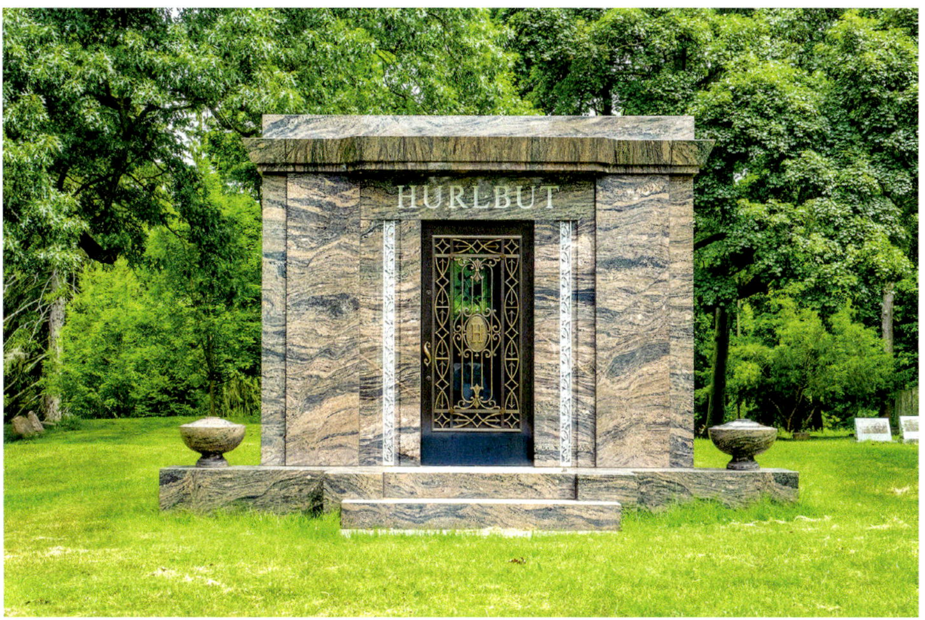

The few new private mausoleums created recently have a contemporary feel. The Hurlburt family mausoleum at Mount Hope is constructed of rainbow granite from Minnesota. Its sharp contours are complemented by the intricate pattern of the door.

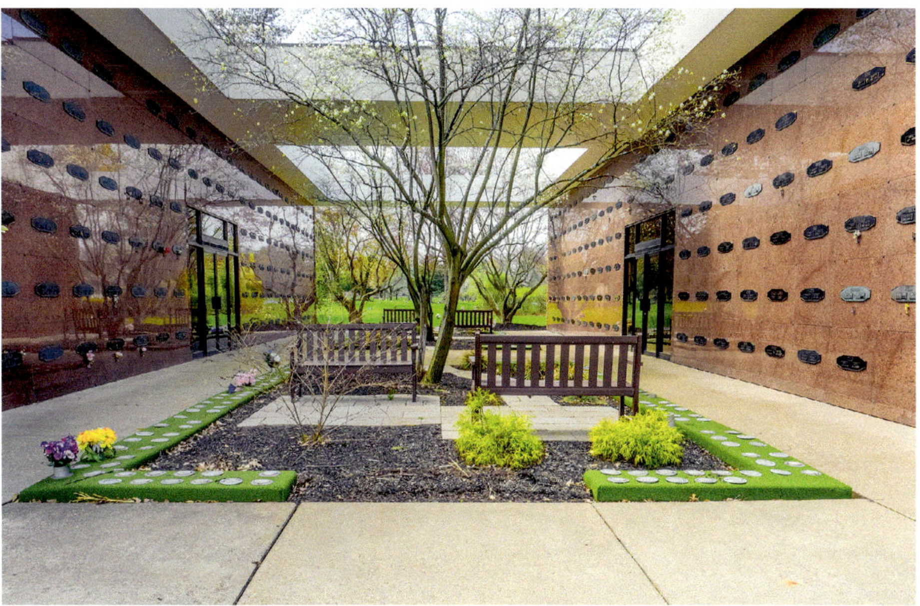

More common in the new century are community mausoleums such as this one at Whitehaven, Pittsford. The vaults are accessible from the outside, eliminating expensive air purifying systems for the building. It has clean contemporary lines. The garden area has space for cremated remains and a sitting area for families.

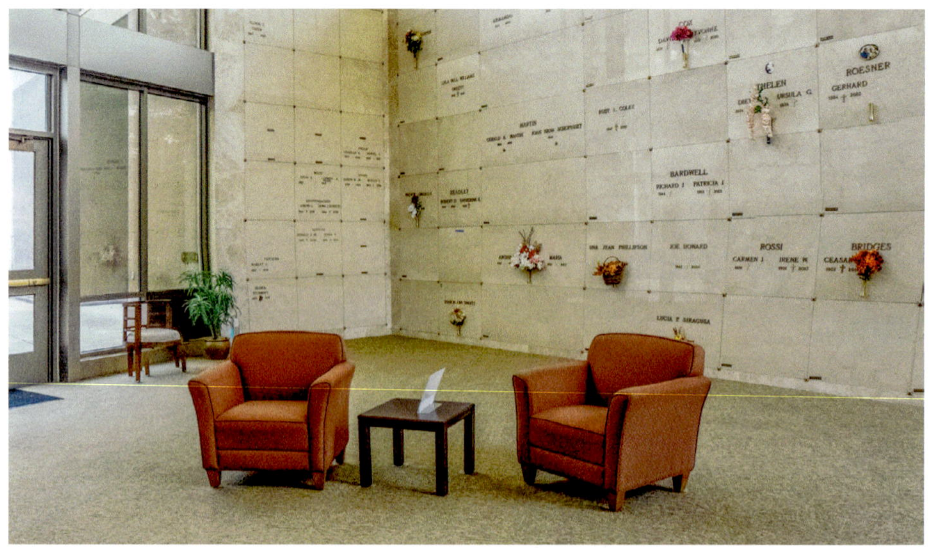

Riverside Cemetery has an imposing group of mausoleum structures near its entrance on Lake Avenue. Attached to the central building is a chapel filled with light.

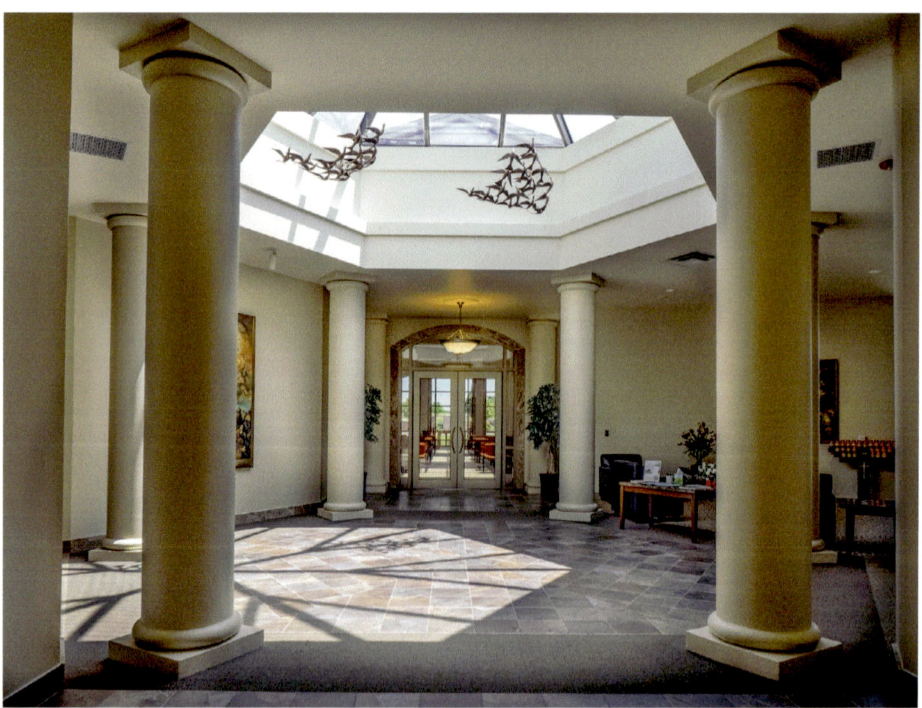

Ascension Gardens, Henrietta, is a recently developed garden cemetery with a vast amount of open land for the future. It offers a variety of interment options including memorial garden spaces, natural green burial options, and this magnificent mausoleum structure with attractive enclosures for cremains.

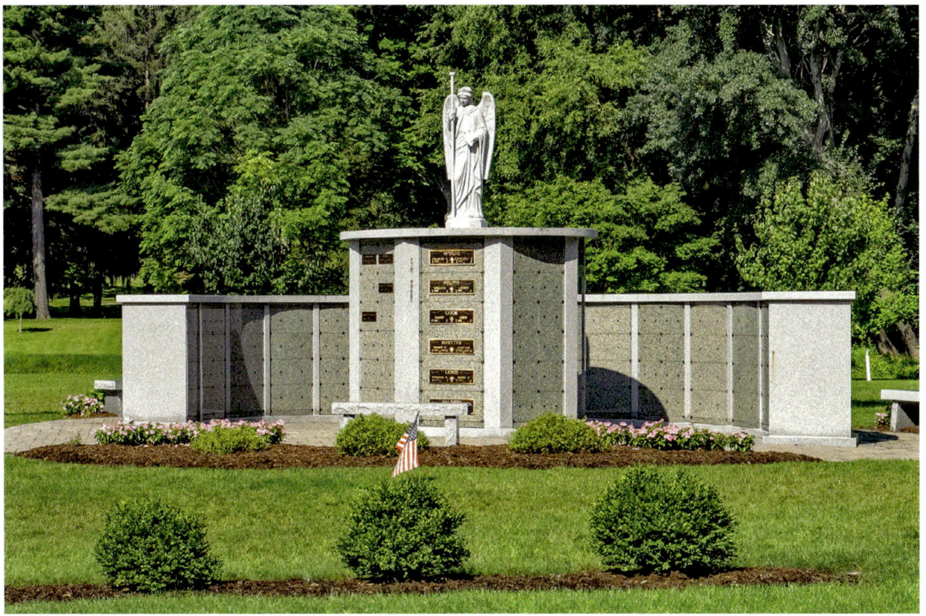

Holy Sepulchre is one of several area cemeteries offering outdoor columbaria in carefully landscaped settings. Cold Spring Cemetery, Lockport, has a similar grouping near its entrance. Sodus Rural, Irondequoit, Riverside, and Webster Union also have added such structures recently. Some 50–60 percent of families now are choosing cremation.

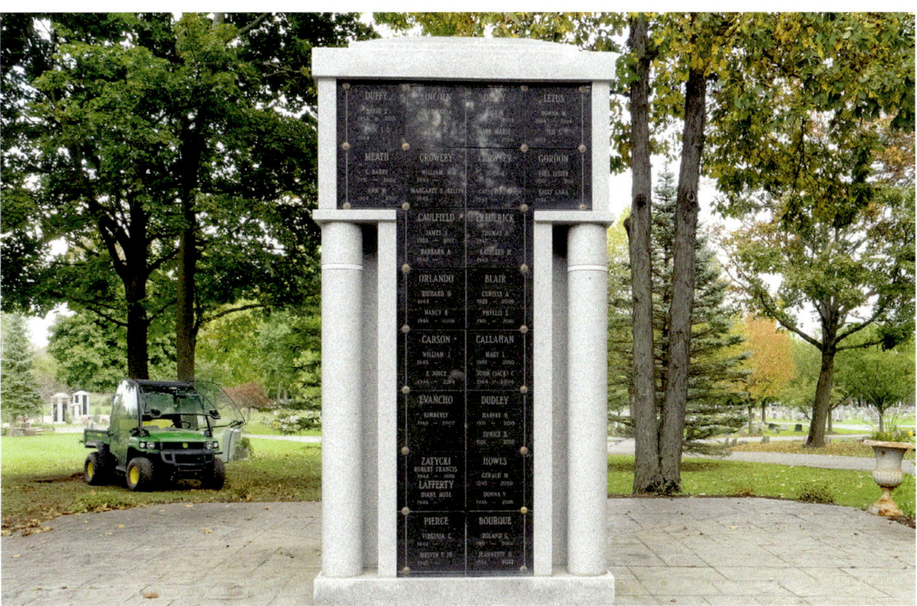

Woodlawn in Canandaigua has found smaller spots where upright structures for cremated remains can be placed amidst existing headstones. Mount Hope is creating spots for similar structures.

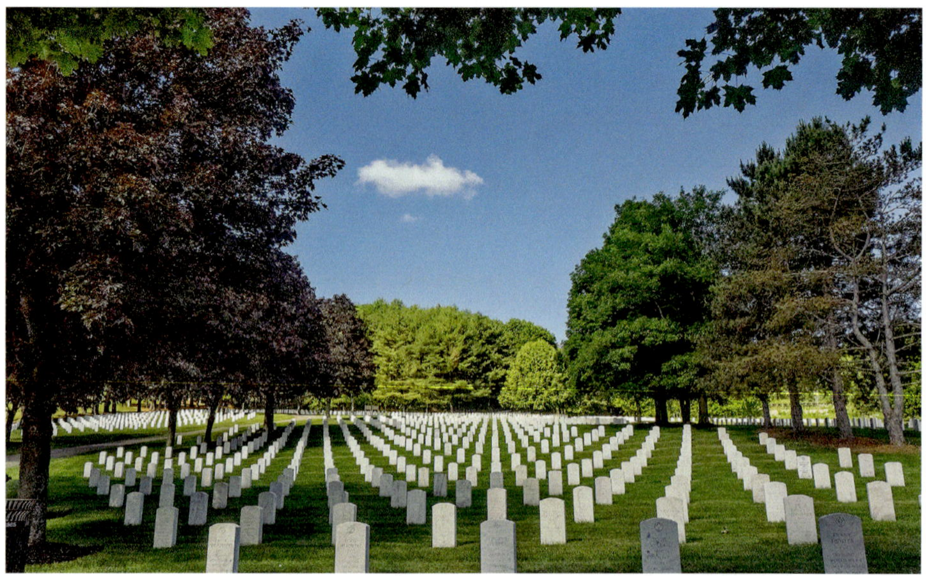

After the Civil War, national military cemeteries were developed to honor veterans. The town of Bath in the southern tier is the site of a large Veterans Administration complex that includes one of the original national burial grounds. The Bath National Cemetery remains active today, opening new areas for recent generations of veterans. It is very moving to see row upon row of white monuments lined up as if they were on parade.

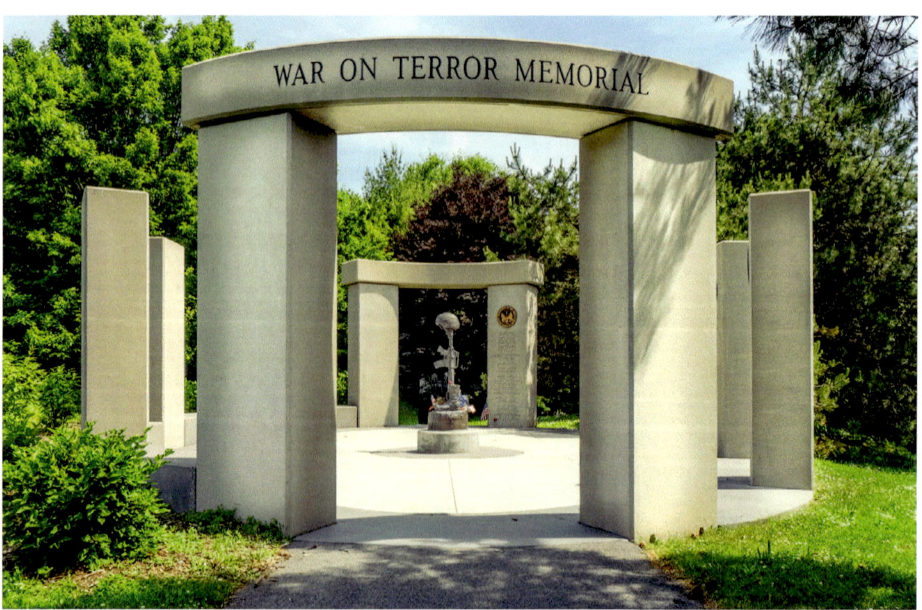

Highland Park South near the Vietnam Memorial in Rochester is the site of a new War on Terror Memorial honoring area soldiers who continue to serve the country around the globe.

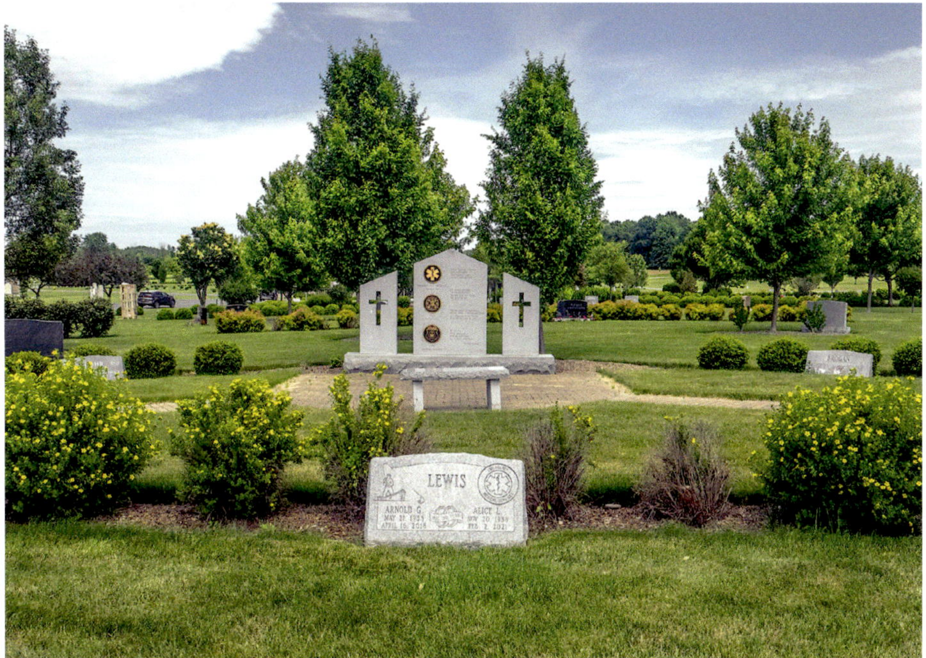

Holy Sepulchre and Ascension Gardens have created monuments to First Responders from police, fire and medical services. This one at Ascension Gardens has a beautiful setting.

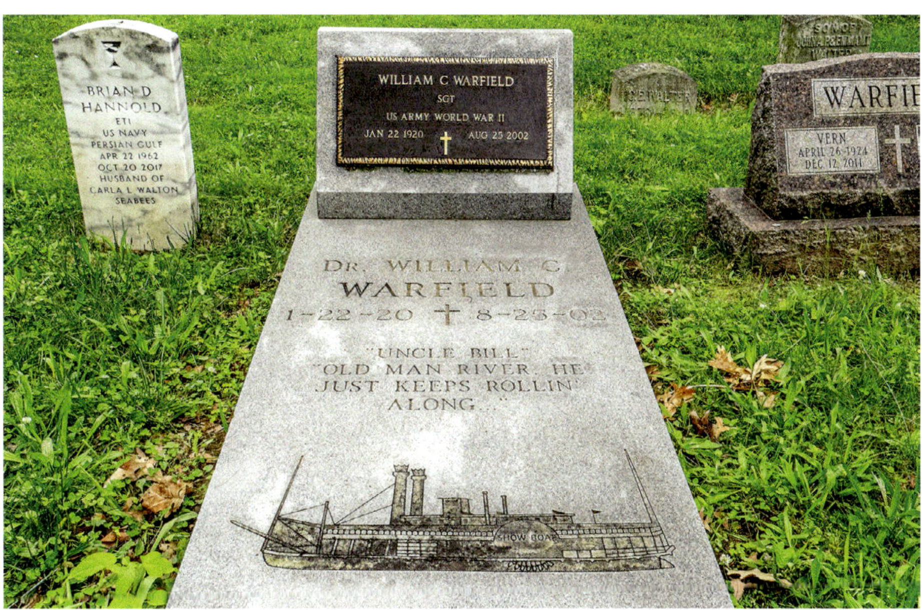

Recently at Mount Hope I happened upon the monument for William Warfield. He fought in World War II and is famous as old Joe in *Show Boat*. For those who have heard it, his rendition of "Ol' Man River" will never be forgotten. His deep bass voice was truly moving and remarkable.

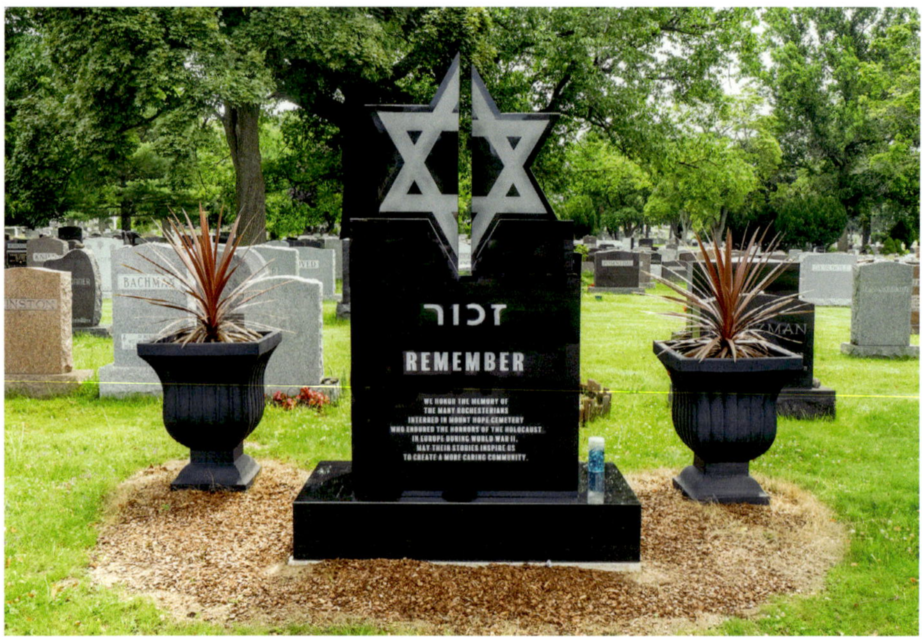

A monument to the survivors of the Holocaust was erected at Mount Hope in 2023. Designed and crafted by Bill Yager, this unique monument is a compelling reminder of the survival of the human spirit amidst unspeakable evil and cruelty.

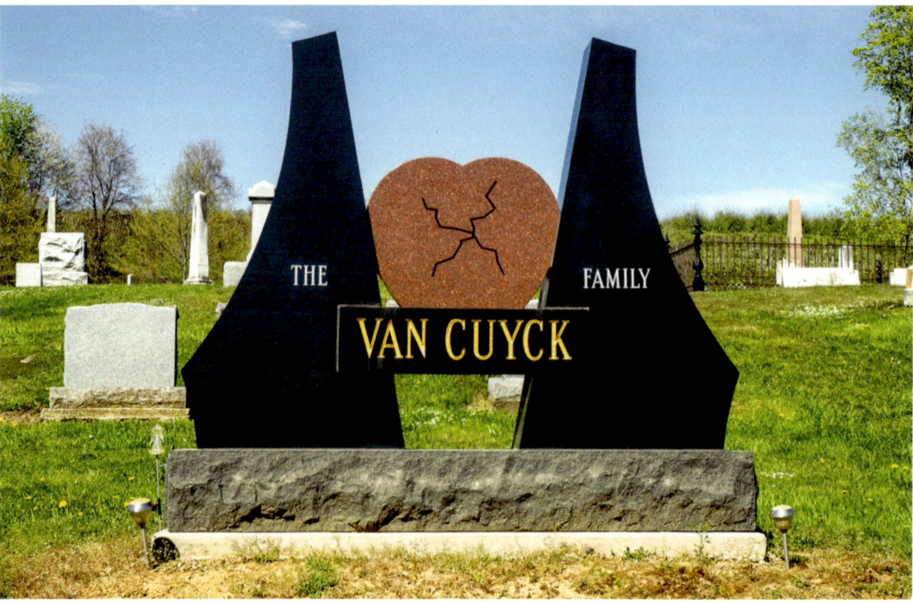

No longer dependent upon local quarries for their raw materials, monument companies now offer a large variety of granite that can be cut into unique shapes and finished with individual designs. This simple yet elegant monument at Sodus Rural Cemetery is arresting.

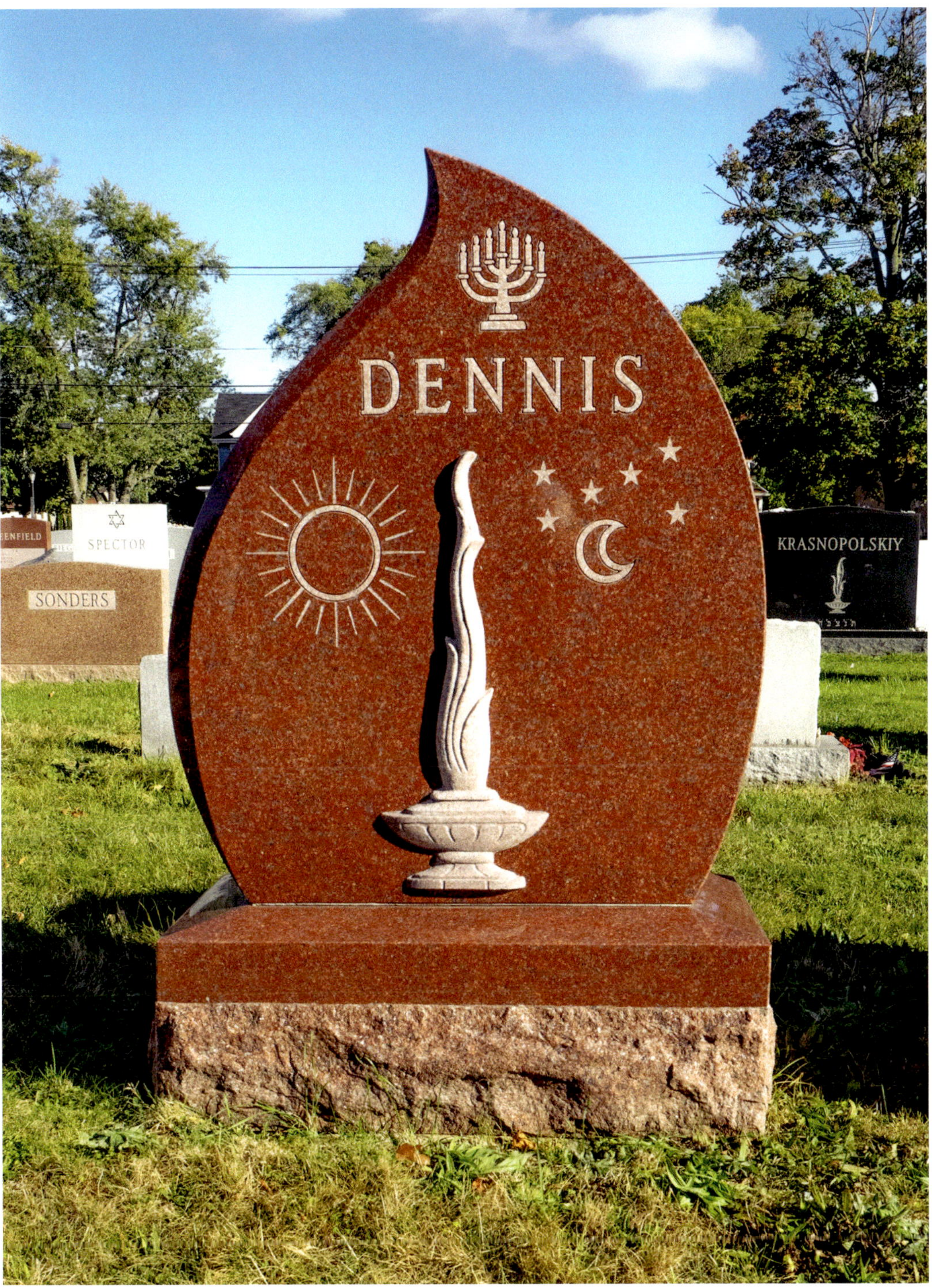

This Mount Hope marker conveys a sense of eternity through a contemporary depiction of inextinguishable flames.

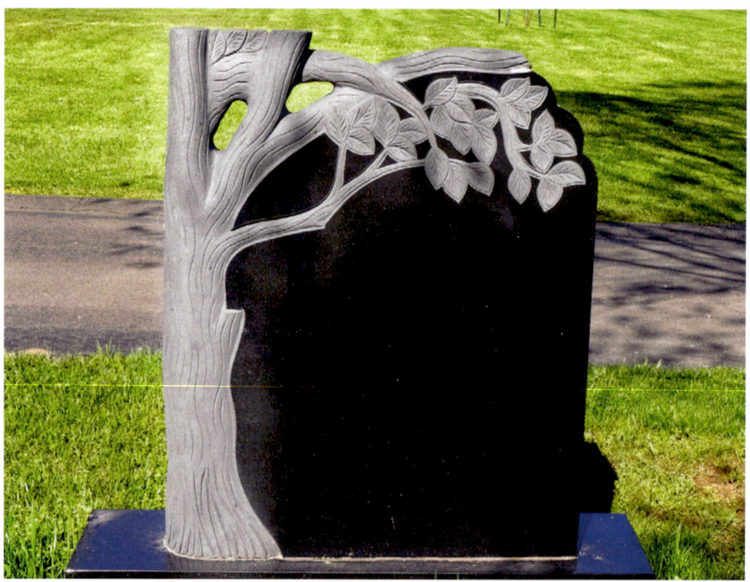

The design of this headstone at Webster Union Cemetery reminds me of the Art Nouveau style popular during the early to mid-twentieth century. As people plan for the future by buying cemetery plots and designing their own headstones, their unfinished markers may await completion of the design until their death. While it is unusual to place a stone with no engraved information, specialists can complete the design at the cemetery at the appropriate time.

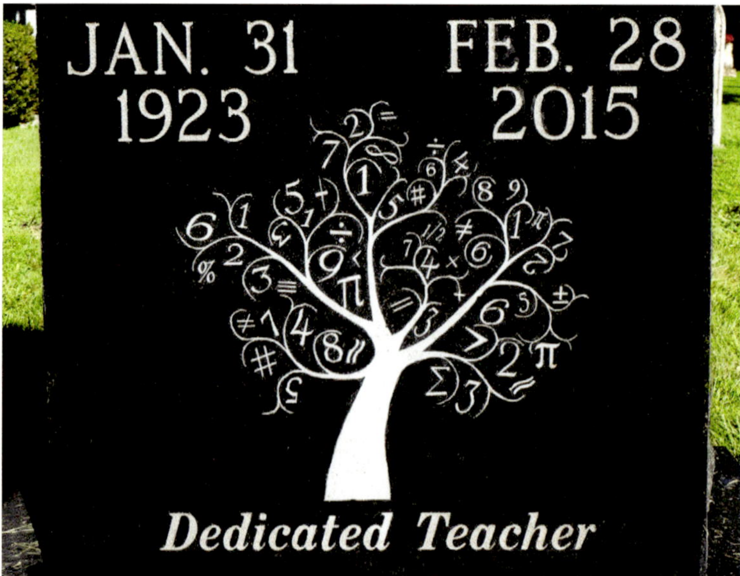

This unique design at Oakwood Cemetery, Penfield, tells the story of the person buried there. Its tree of life is filled with math symbols and other notations that form a permanent record of the individual's journey through life.

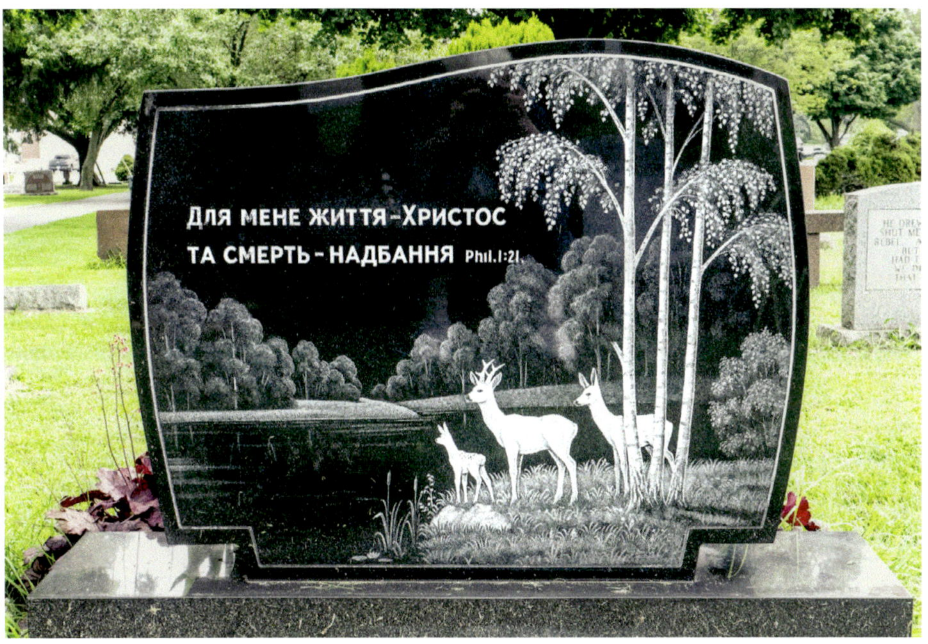

Granite can be sand blasted, laser etched, or hand engraved. On black stone the image and letters are painted to create a long-lasting, highly visible design. This headstone at Falls Cemetery, Greece is an impressive example.

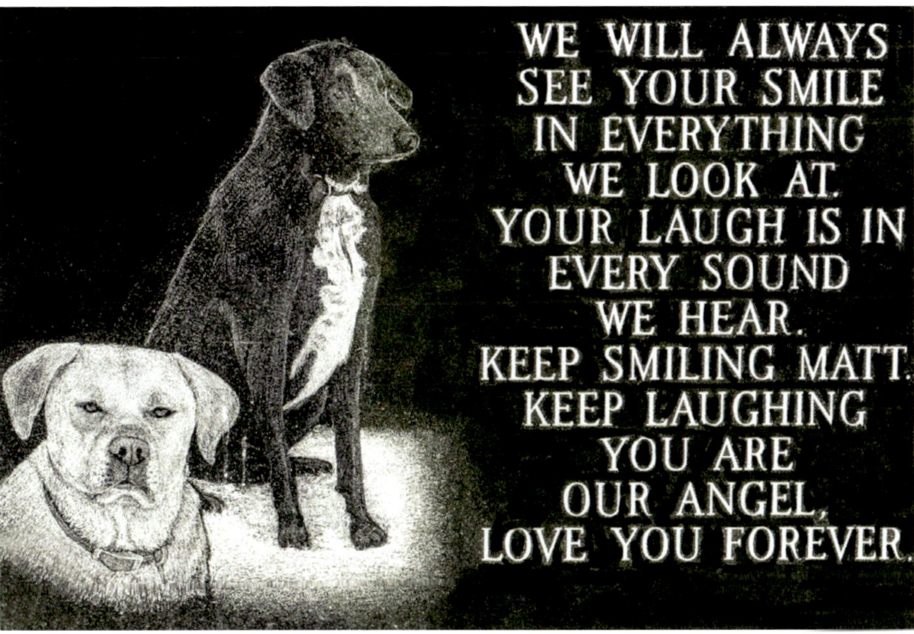

This Webster Rural Cemetery headstone combines artwork created from a photograph with a thoughtful epitaph.

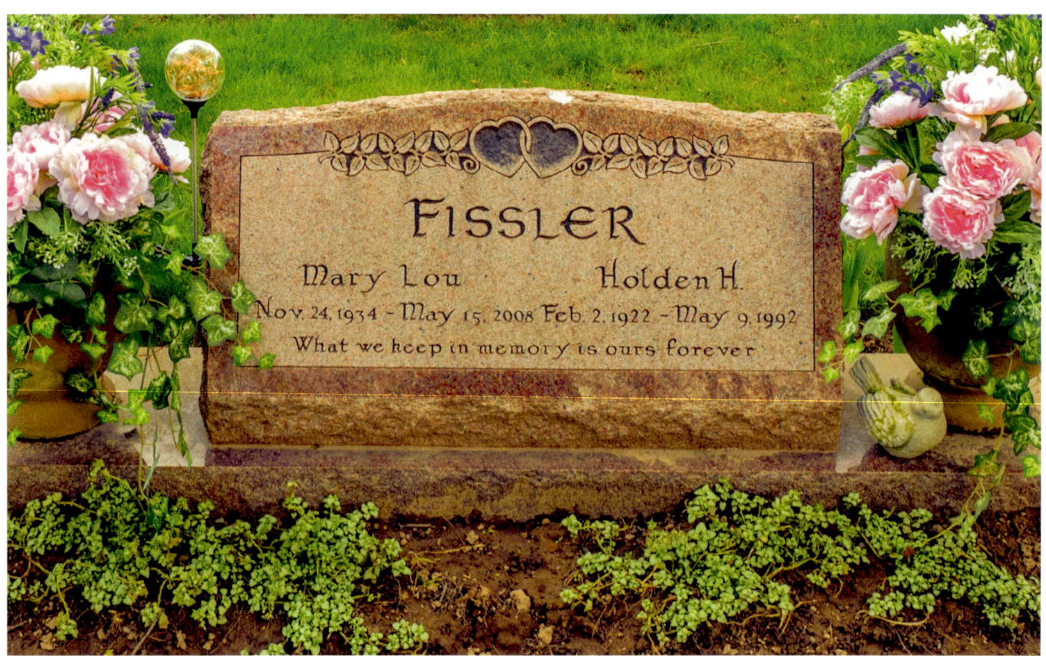

The slant-front headstone design continues to be a popular memorial form. Each has space for personalization. Each tells a story of someone's life, or family history, or place in the community. These two stones from Garland Cemetery, Brockport (above) and Webster Union Cemetery (below) convey the love and care they represent. Spring flowers and fall decorations bring life to the gravesite. It becomes a place to share memories with family and friends, a place of beauty and solace.

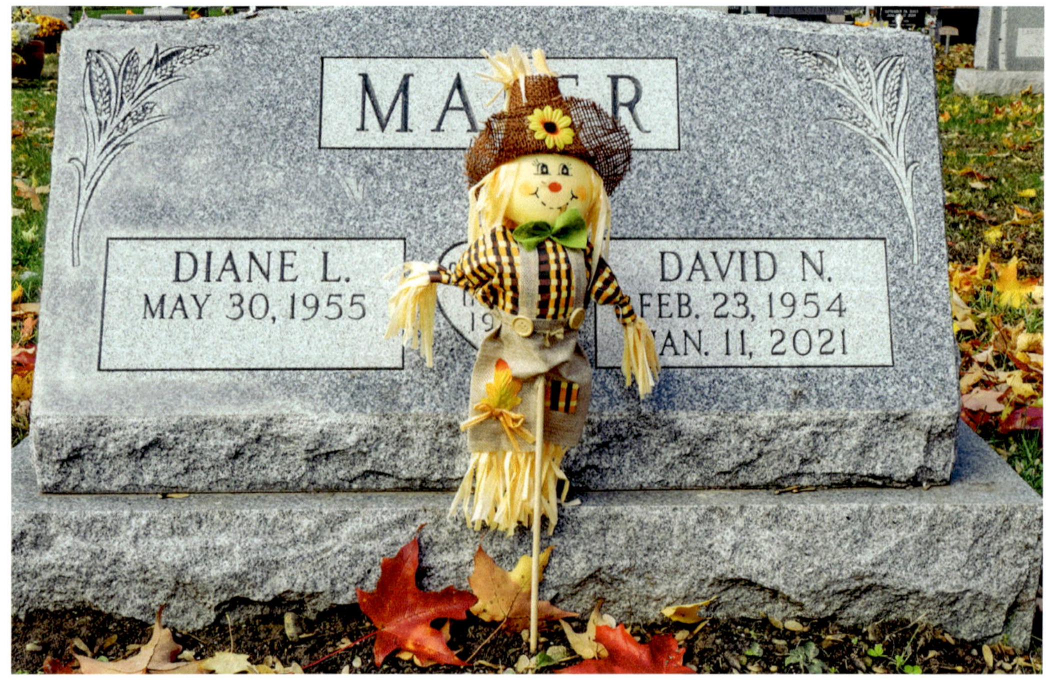

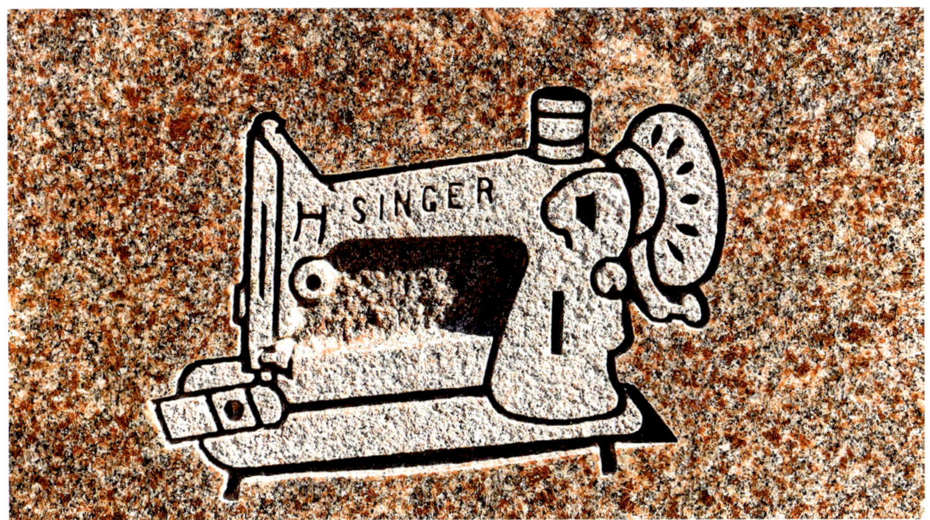

Whether a headstone is large or small, current technology allows for the engraving of symbols of the deceased's interests and activities. I met a neighbor at Webster Union Cemetery whose wife recently had died. She had been an avid seamstress, and her talents were lovingly memorialized by her family in the design.

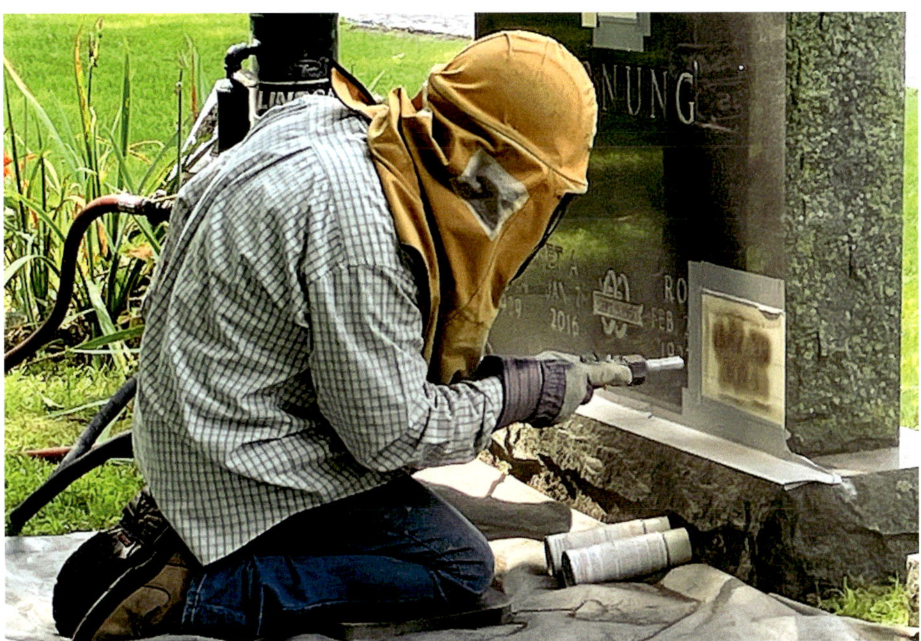

Many headstones are placed in a cemetery prior to the death of a spouse or partner left behind. The date can be added to the headstone later onsite by a specialist. At the cemetery, an appropriate stencil of the design and/or personal information is sandblasted onto the headstone with care and precision. In this image the final death date is etched into the stone. Before the stencil is removed, the can of paint on the ground will be used to spray the design white on the black granite.

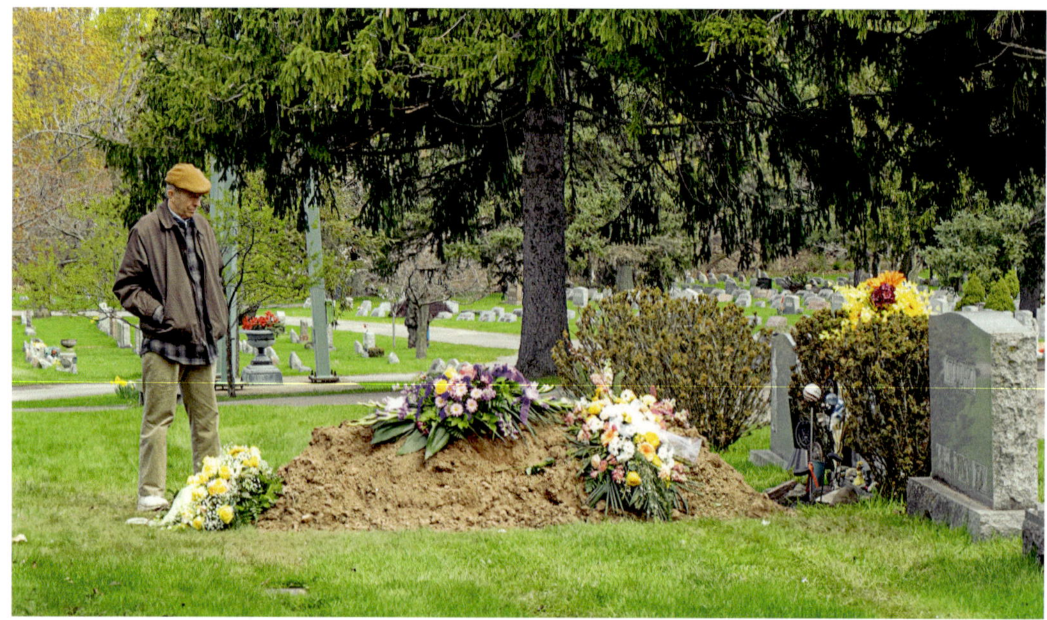

The pandemic brought death to the forefront as families experienced an epidemic not seen for over a century. Grief, often private in the past, became a shared community experience. Visitors brought cemeteries to new life as loved ones were mourned. Soil generally is mounded over the grave to allow for settling. The placement of flowers on or beside the grave follows a centuries-old tradition. Flowers acknowledge grief and loss. Ancient Romans believed that flowers and mementos showed departed spirits they were not forgotten. Early religious rites used flowers to commemorate the cycle of life.

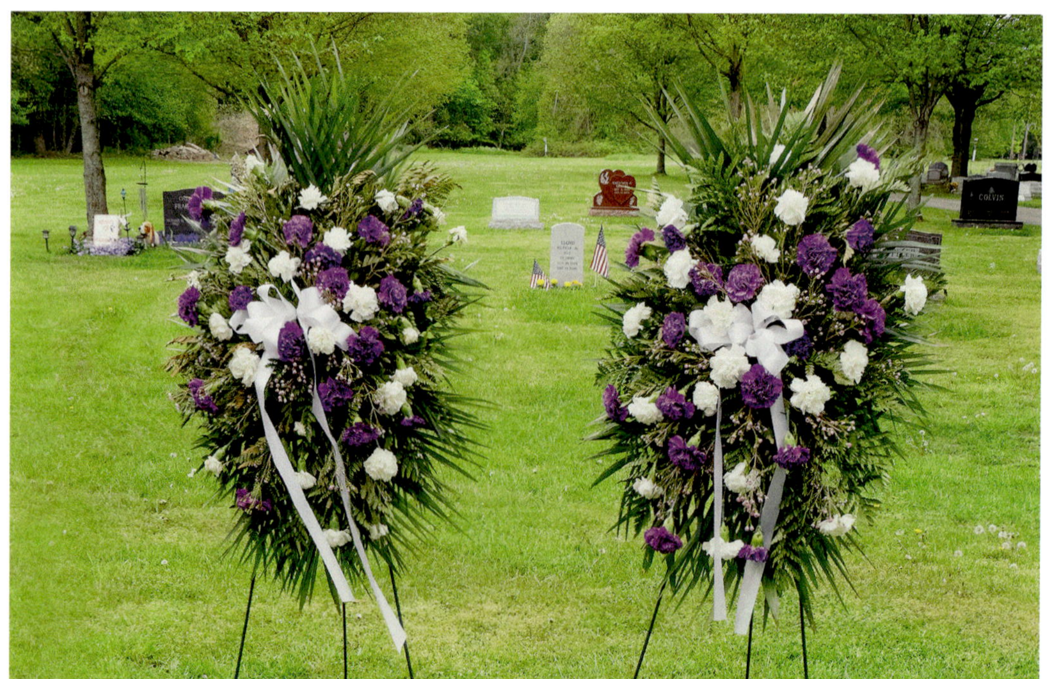

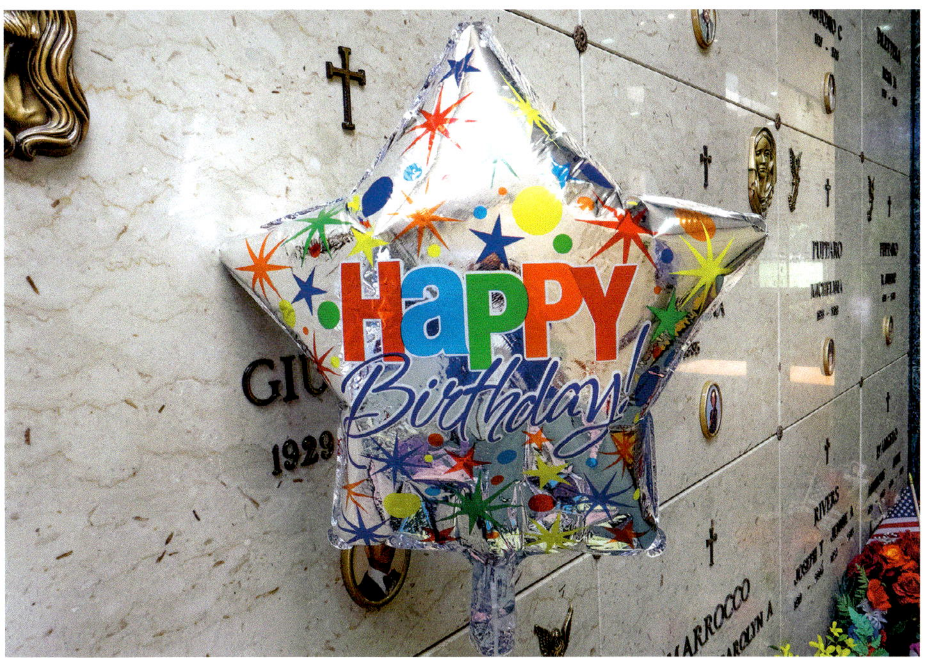

The cemetery is an important meeting place for the living and the dead. Birthdays, anniversaries, and holidays can be celebrated at the gravesite, mausoleum, or columbarium. Often, colorful decorations appear marking these special events. Honoring such dates helps keep memories alive, partially filling the void left by a missing place at the table. No matter the interment method, people are not forgotten.

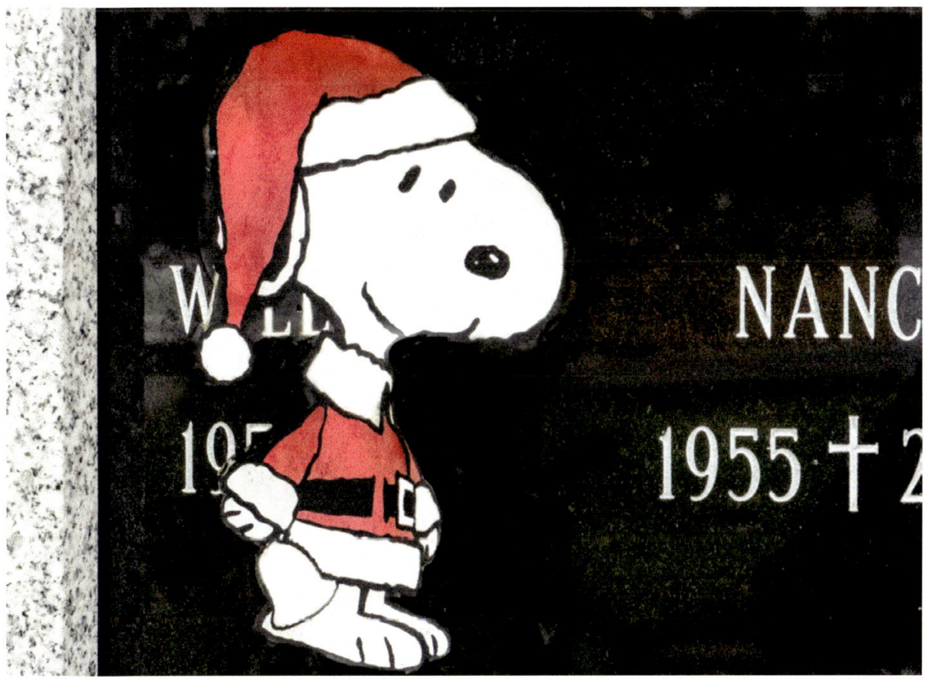

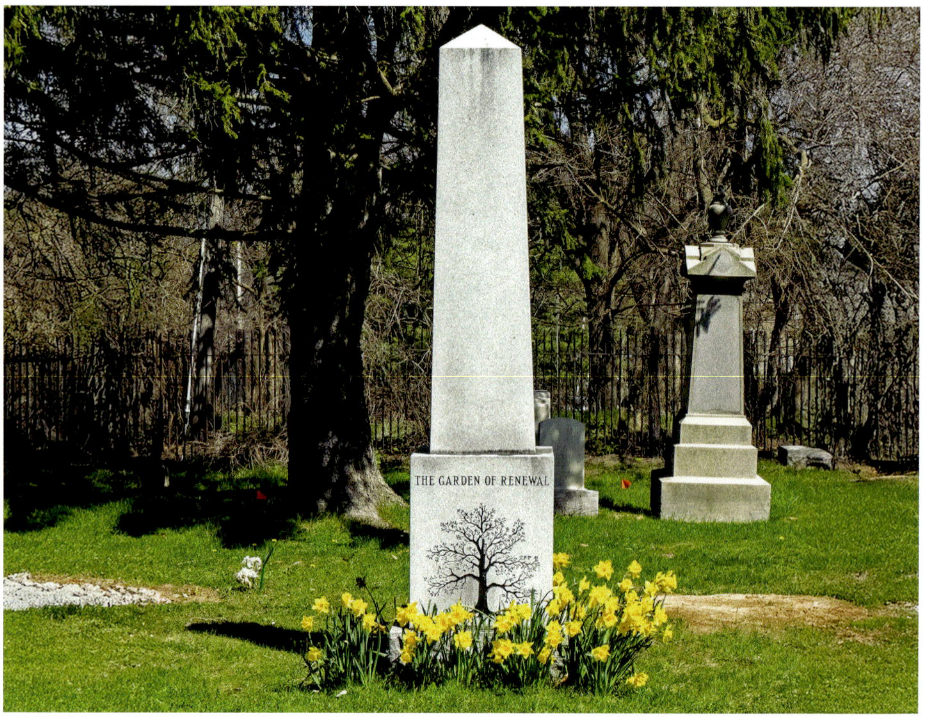

Traditional cemeteries are responding to new trends. Mount Hope is an example of changes being made at many area cemeteries. A memorial scattering garden (above) has been created overlooking an old part of the cemetery near the North Gate. The tree of life (below) adorns the central marker in a new green burial section at the very north end of the cemetery.

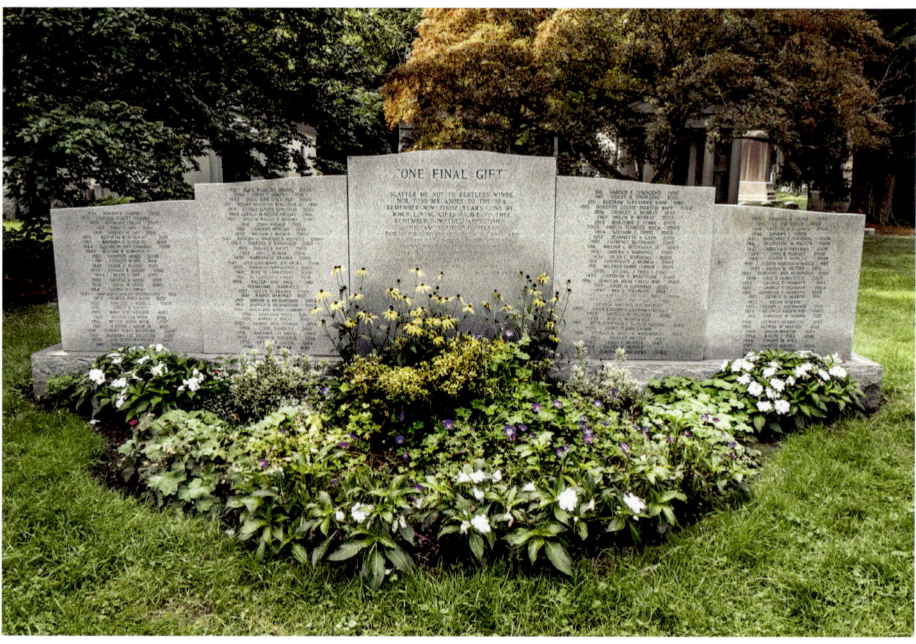

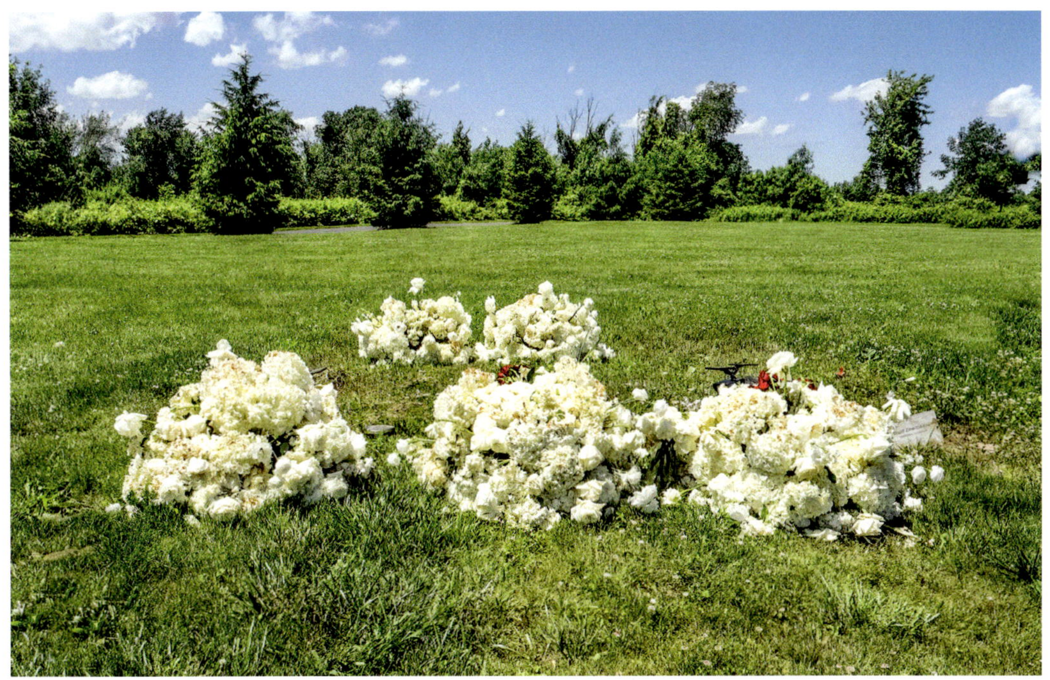

Two relatively new cemeteries have been created in the area. The Avon Muslim Cemetery was developed in the year 2000. Located in a lovely upstate setting, five graves (above) are covered with beautiful fresh flowers overlooking an area set aside for those to come. Ascension Gardens, Rush (below), reflects the need for more space and new interment options as burial traditions evolve.

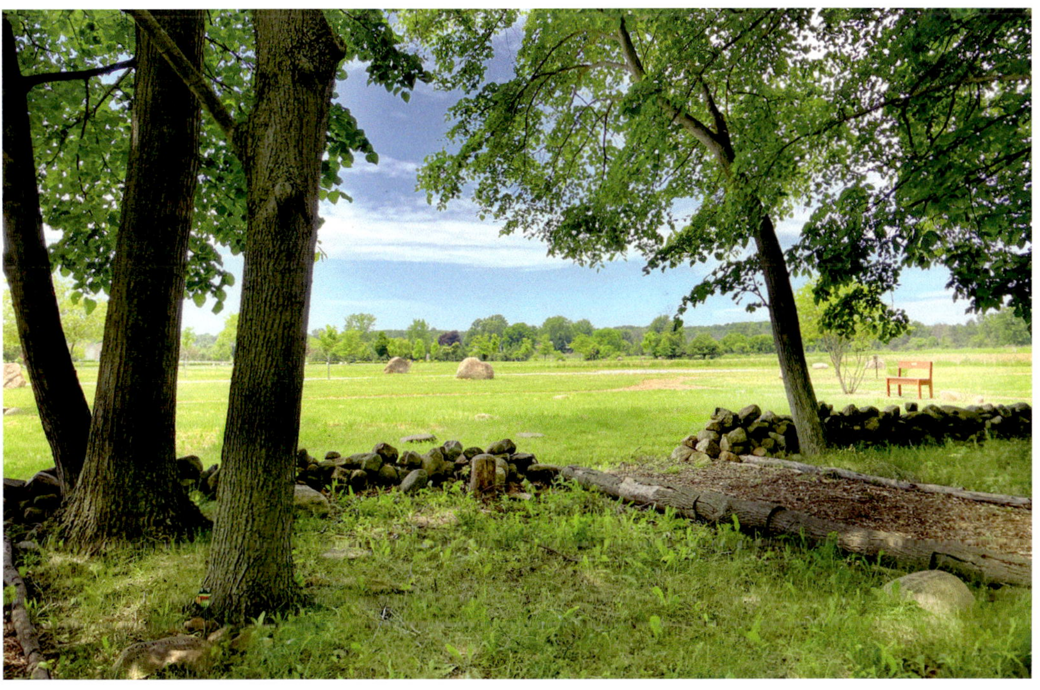

4

Cemetery Landscape in Context

The Rochester area is particularly inviting for exploring cemetery geology, flora, and fauna. Geologists come to local cemeteries to study our unique underlying glacial formations. Rochester's Ellwanger-Barry Nursery was by 1855 the country's largest, and it contributed lovely and unusual plantings to local cemeteries. There now are over 100 different species of trees at Mount Hope. It, along with Whitehaven Memorial Garden, is a certified wildlife habitat.

Surrounding towns have equally interesting cemeteries—some near the Erie Canal, some overlooking agricultural fields, wineries and orchards. Others celebrate changing seasons or highlight the history and hopes of the people who settled here.

Although cemeteries can be regarded as cities of the dead, they are alive with the history of their towns. As the calendar moves us forward, it is important to remember our roots and preserve our history.

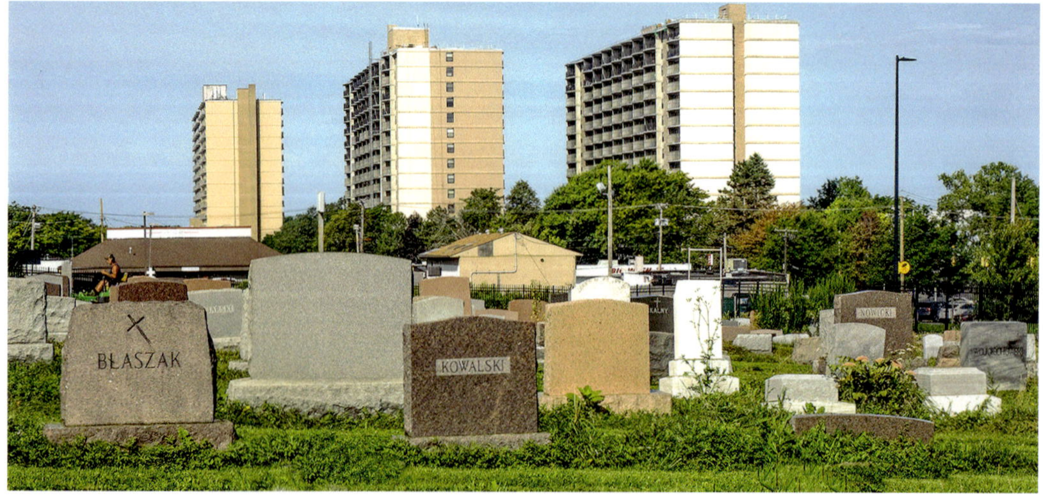

Irondequoit's Saint Casimir Cemetery, created 120 years ago, is a quiet reminder of the past. Hemmed in by Route 104, Walmart Plaza, and large apartment buildings, it silently watches as twenty-first-century life bustles by.

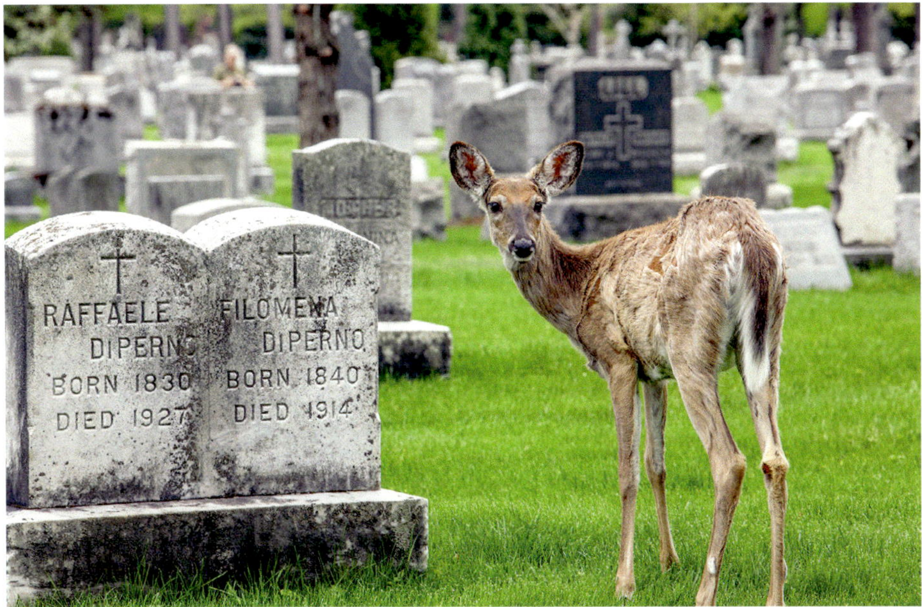

Spotting wildlife while wandering through a cemetery is a lovely surprise. All kinds of creatures find their way into these quiet places away from the bustle of cars and people. Black cats seem to abound. Gophers and badgers have homes under headstones. Deer are a welcome sight at Mount Hope, and at Holy Sepulchre deer often appear in the northwest part of the newer section. Birds and small mammals seek homes and protection in the trees and bushes. Whitehaven and Mount Hope are certified Audubon sanctuaries.

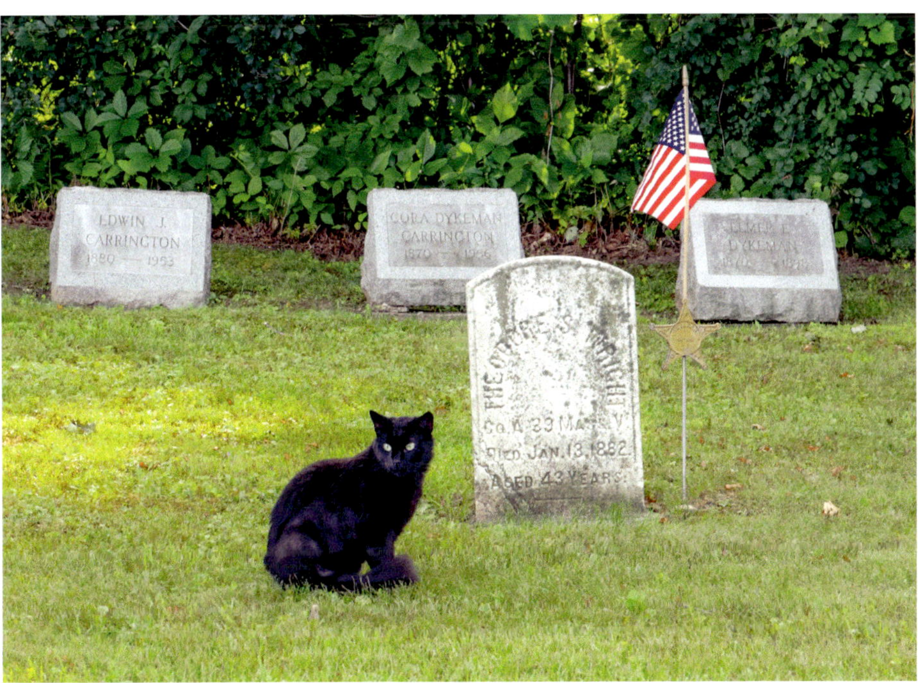

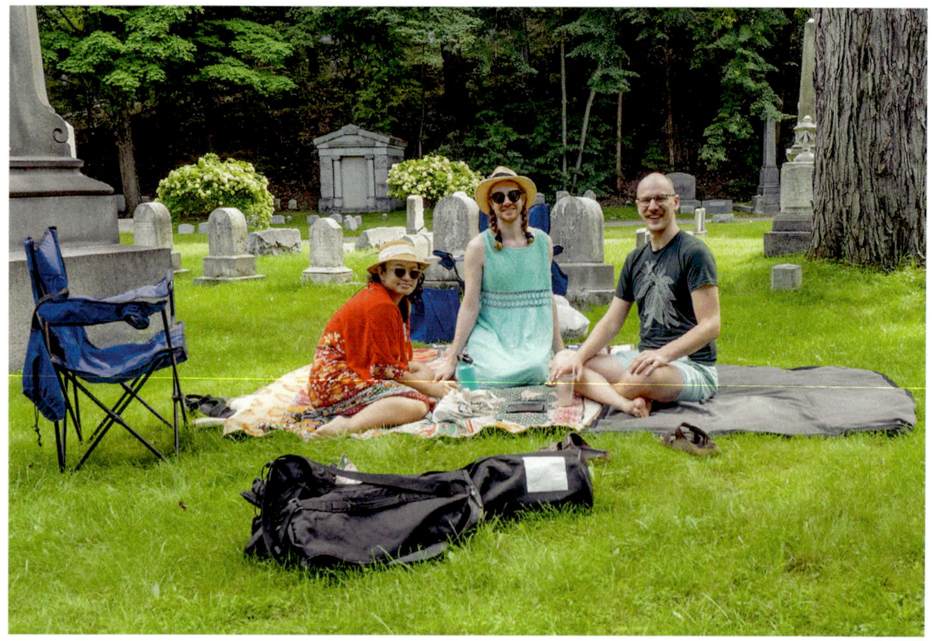

In Victorian times, families would take picnic lunches to the cemetery to be with their loved ones surrounded by inviting scenery. This newly married couple decided to celebrate with their friend in a quiet spot one beautiful day at Mount Hope. Their festive air calls to mind those happy Victorian outings.

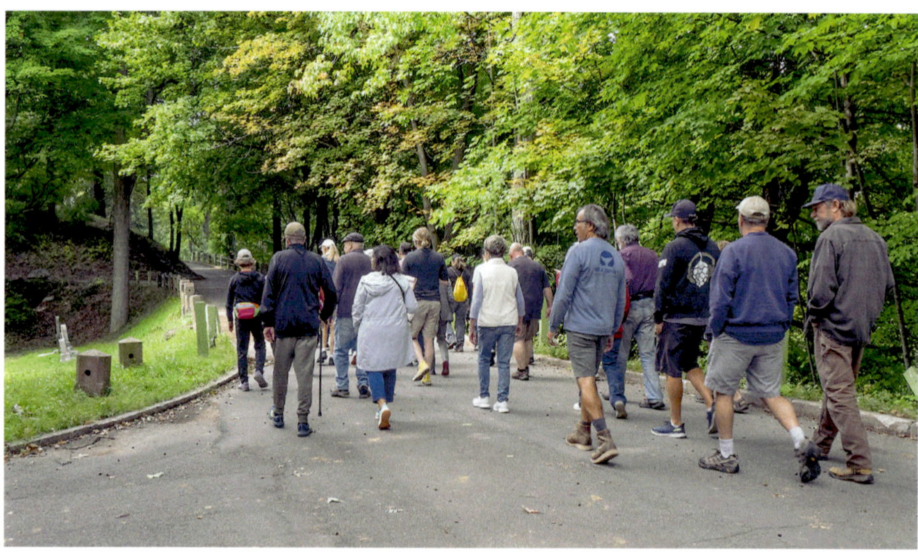

Tours enrich the cemetery experience. They create a broader context, enlivening history, and highlighting landscapes that might otherwise go unnoticed. Mount Hope has numerous tours during the year led by knowledgeable volunteers. Both local and out-of-town visitors explore family genealogies and the diverse significance of our "residents."

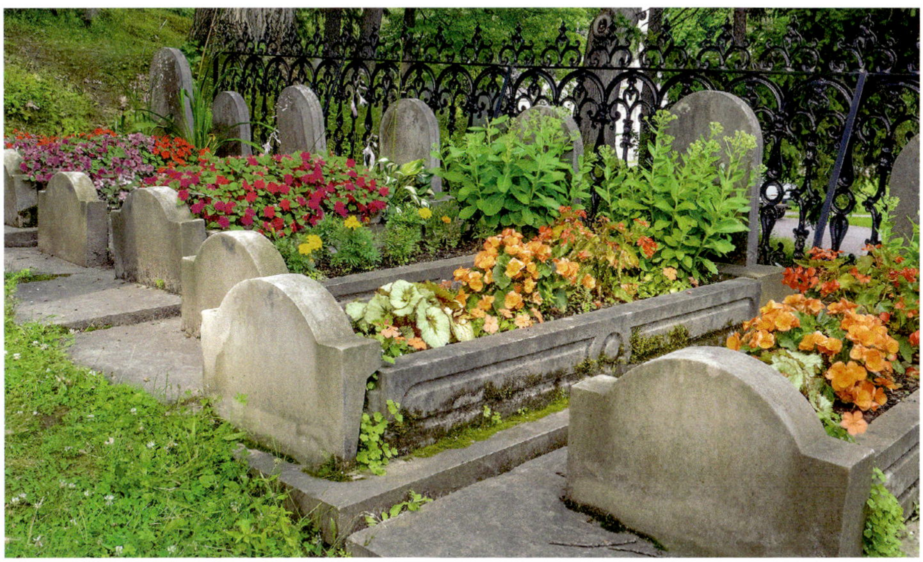

Dedicated volunteers make an enormous difference in the life of a cemetery. Recently the Friends of Boxwood Cemetery in Medina sponsored a fundraising afternoon tea. Later in the summer, a restoration workshop was held. Friends of Mount Hope (FOMH) annually pairs cradle graves with individuals whose artful plantings restore these graves' poignant allure.

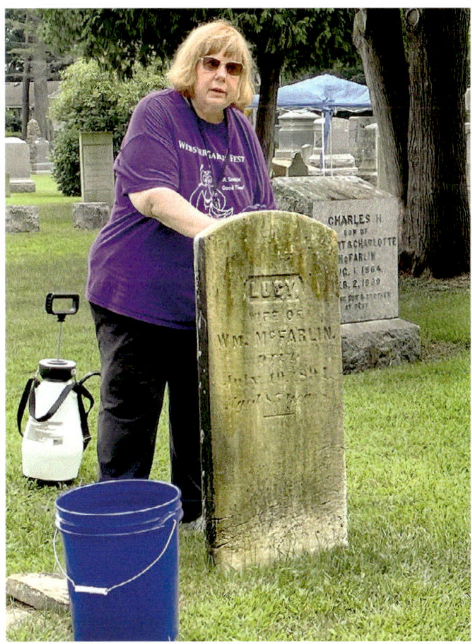

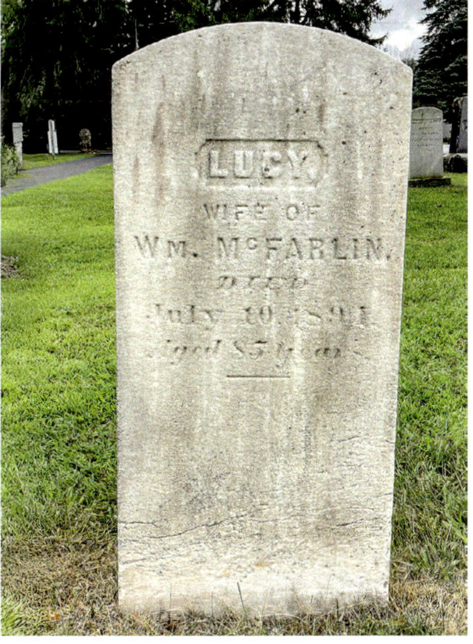

Historic events are celebrated in ways that foster a sense of community. Webster Union Cemetery marked its 200th anniversary in 2024 with vignettes of early settlers and displays of cemetery-related information. A headstone cleaning workshop demonstrated an easy and safe way to restore early marble stones. Cemetery historian Cherie Wood's efforts yielded the improvements shown in these two images.

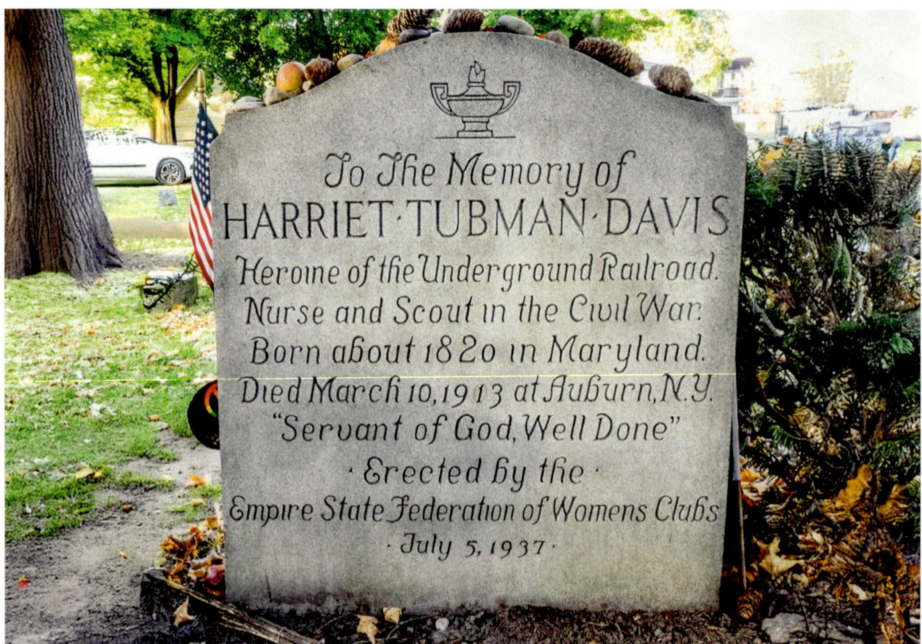

Harriet Tubman Davis, former slave, Underground Railroad conductor, Civil War scout and nurse, is buried in section West Lawn C at Fort Hill Cemetery, Auburn (above). While at the cemetery, look also for the family monuments of Secretary of State William Seward, whose home was a stop on the Underground Railroad. After leaving Auburn, visit Bushnell Cemetery, Sodus. You will find the grave of Captain George Garlock, who ferried escaping slaves to freedom in Canada on his schooner the *Free Trader*. Back in Rochester, visit Brighton Cemetery, where the Bloss family monument is just to the right of the entrance. A member of the New York Assembly, William Bloss worked for desegregated public schools in Rochester and opened the family home as a safe house for the Underground Railroad.

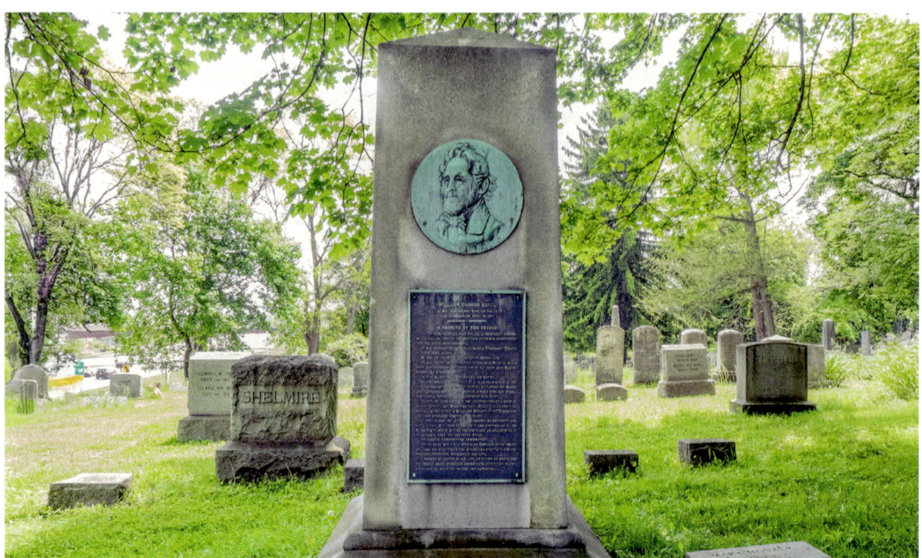

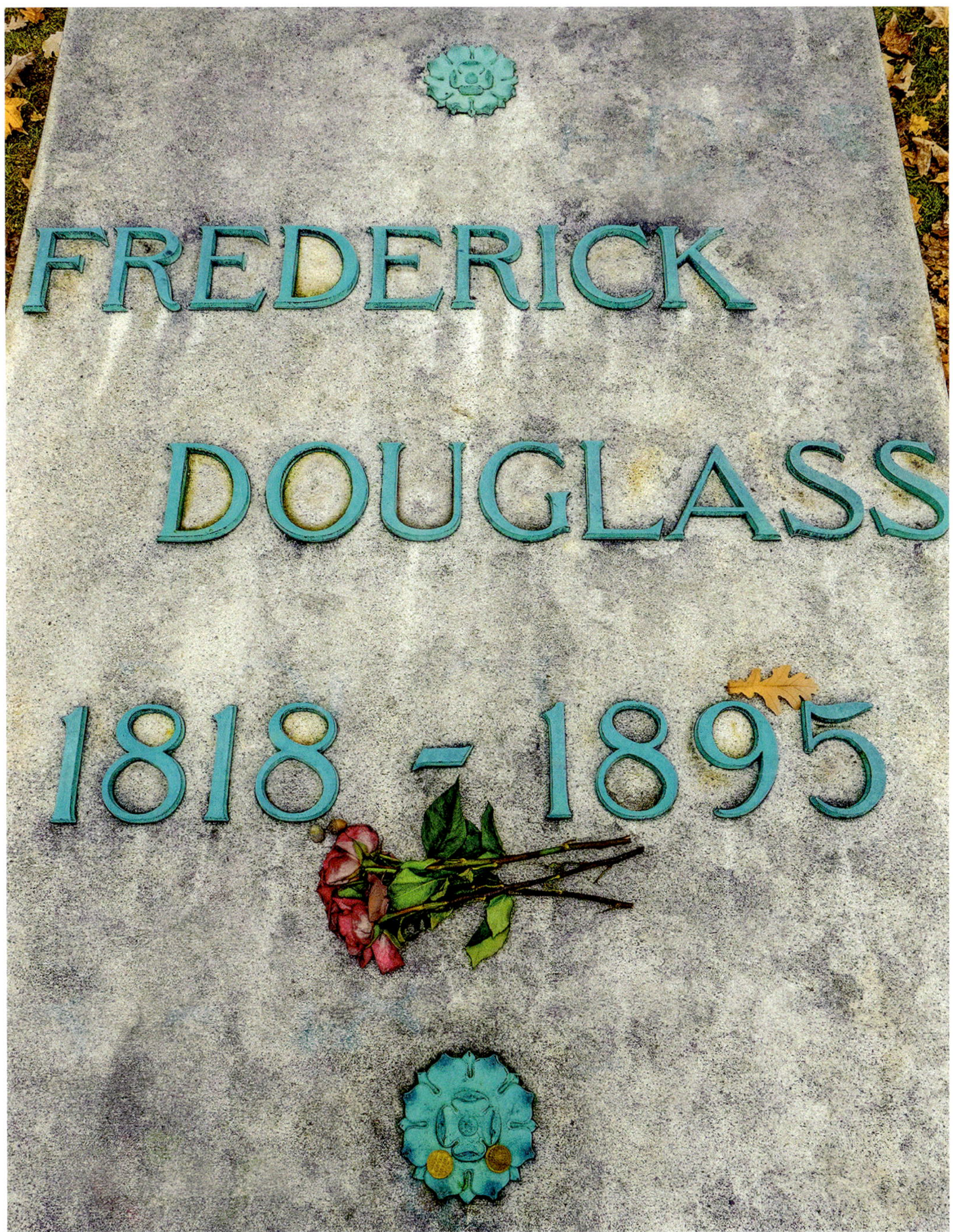

One of the most prominent Mount Hope residents is former slave and leader of the civil rights movement Frederick Douglass. Author, publisher, and active in the Underground Railroad, he worked tirelessly to promote the cause of freedom. A renowned orator, Douglass delivered powerful speeches such as "What to the Slave Is the Fourth of July?" He advised President Lincoln on civil rights issues and worked with his friend Susan B. Anthony for women's suffrage.

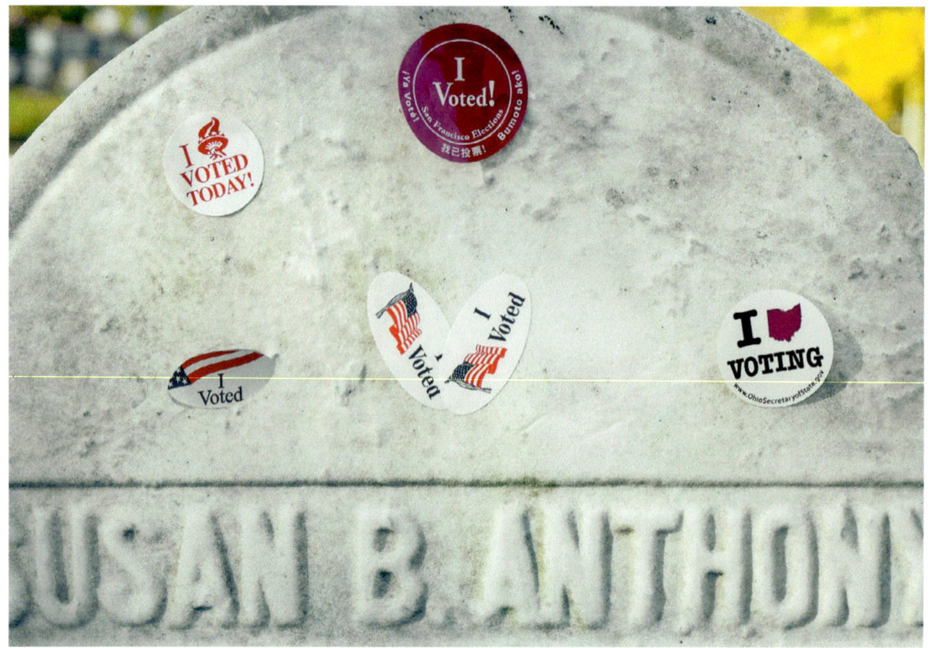

Election Day is a favorite time for people to visit the grave of Susan B. Anthony. In 2020, I was one of the first to leave my "I voted" sticker at her grave (above), celebrating 100 years of the right of women to vote. The gravesite now draws so many visitors on election day that a clear plastic cover (below) has been added to protect the fragile marble from voting sticker glue. The 2023 election cover is on display at the north gatehouse, open during many of the tours.

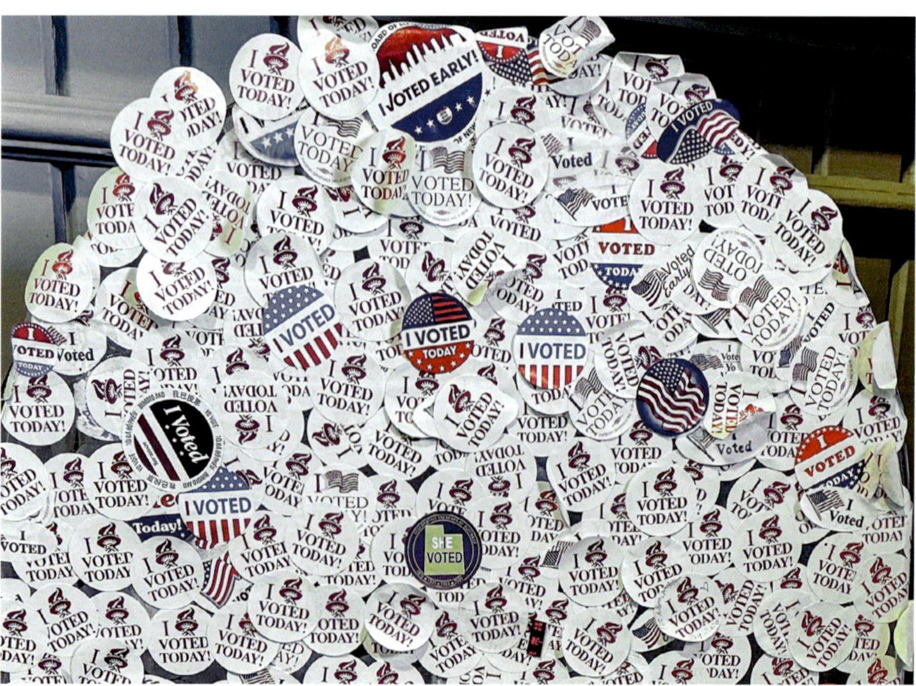

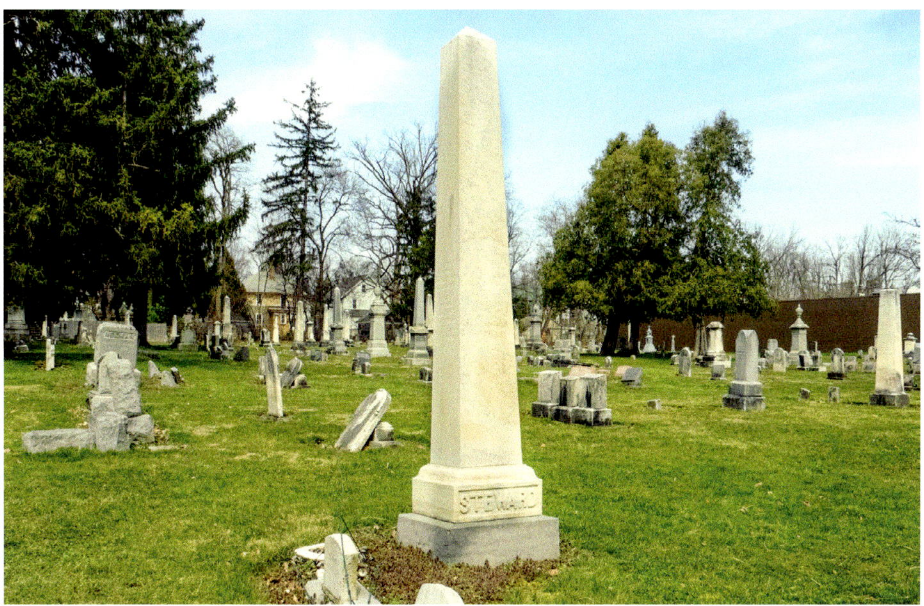

Older burying grounds, such as these in Canandaigua and Brockport, become integral parts of the towns that grow around them. Both have similarly styled marble monuments. Although some are difficult to read after the wear and tear of so many years, they present satisfying rewards for persistence in researching cemetery history. Austin Steward (above), a former slave, Rochester business owner, and author of the book *Twenty-two Years a Slave and Forty Years a Freeman*, is buried with his wife, Patience, and children at West Street Cemetery, Canandaigua. Capt. Joseph Roby (High Street Cemetery, Brockport, below) took part in the Boston Tea Party and fought at Lexington and Concord and Bunker Hill. He died in 1836 after moving to the area upon the death of his wife in Massachusetts.

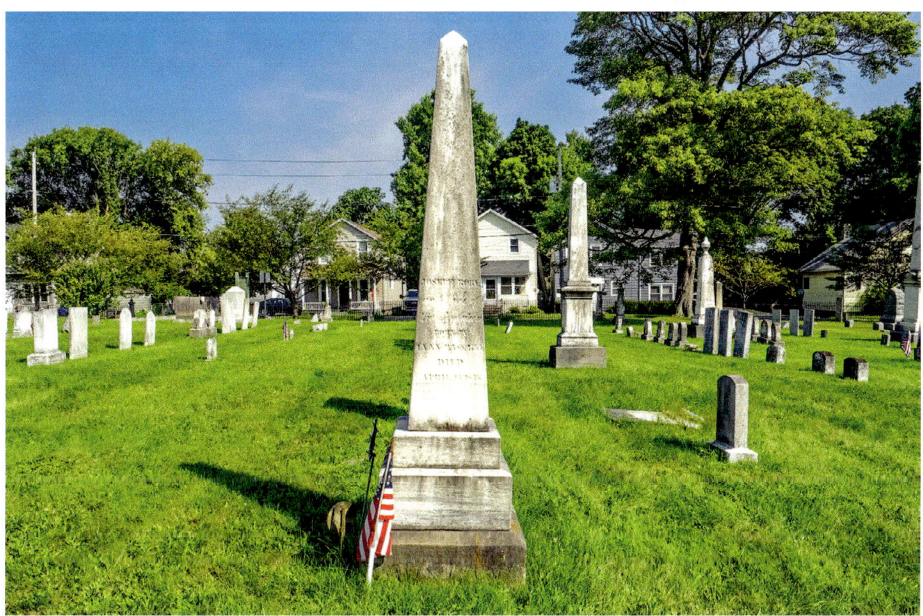

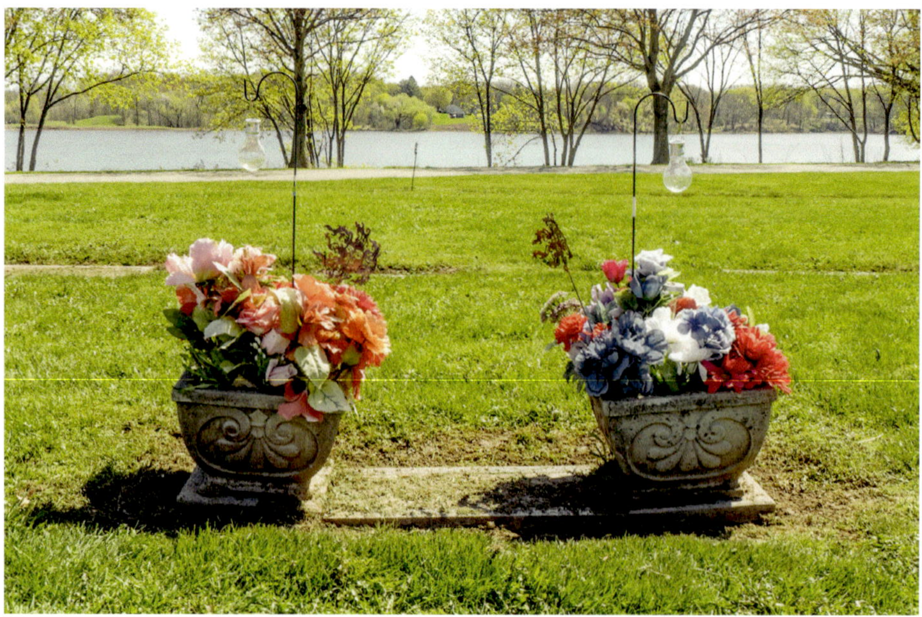

In the early 1800s as towns prospered along the Erie Canal, cemeteries followed. Larger towns created garden cemeteries after the fashion of Mount Hope, each with its own character. Boxwood Cemetery in Medina was so designed. As it grew, flat lawn sections were added. A contemporary area faces Glenwood Lake, formed by a tributary that crosses under the canal south of the cemetery.

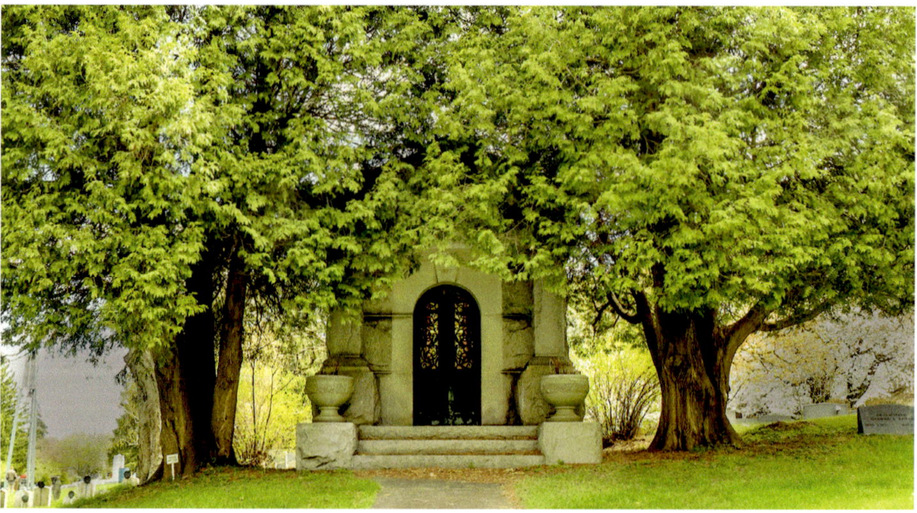

Lockport has a sophisticated multi-level set of canal locks well worth seeing. Next to the canal is the Erie Canal Museum, highly recommended. Created nearby in 1841, Cold Spring Cemetery has cherry trees whose spring blossoms are beautiful. The Lydia and Edwin Carl Mausoleum is dwarfed by northern white cedar trees. Ancient Egyptians believed such trees represent immortality and used the resin for embalming and the wood as coffin liners.

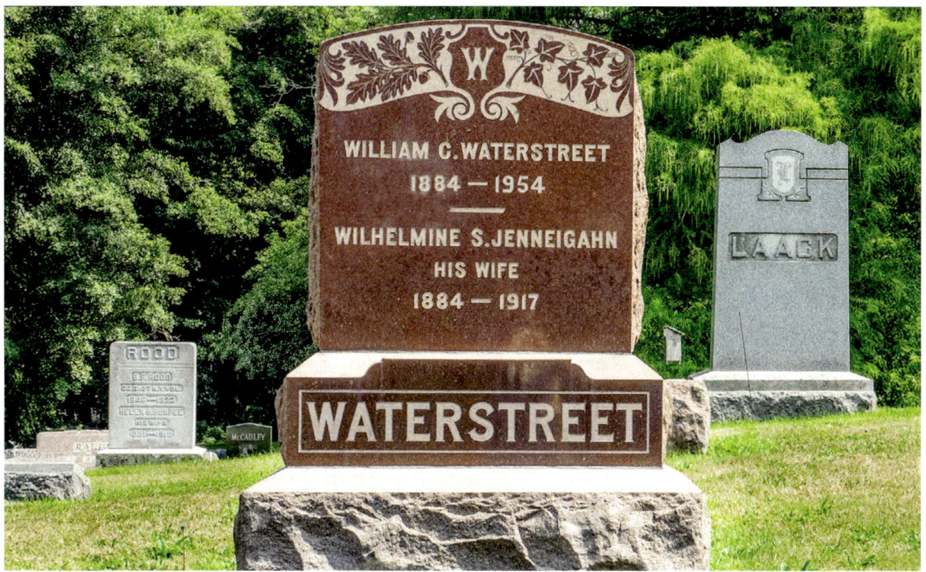

The canal town of Brockport has two cemeteries, High Street in town and garden-style Lakeview Cemetery just outside of town in Sweden. Lakeview has been enlarged to include a modern section pleasantly arrayed on gentle slopes. The Waterstreet family monument has a polished face and rough-hewn sides. The oak and ivy leaves seen here are often portrayed together, symbolizing immutable friendship and lasting memory.

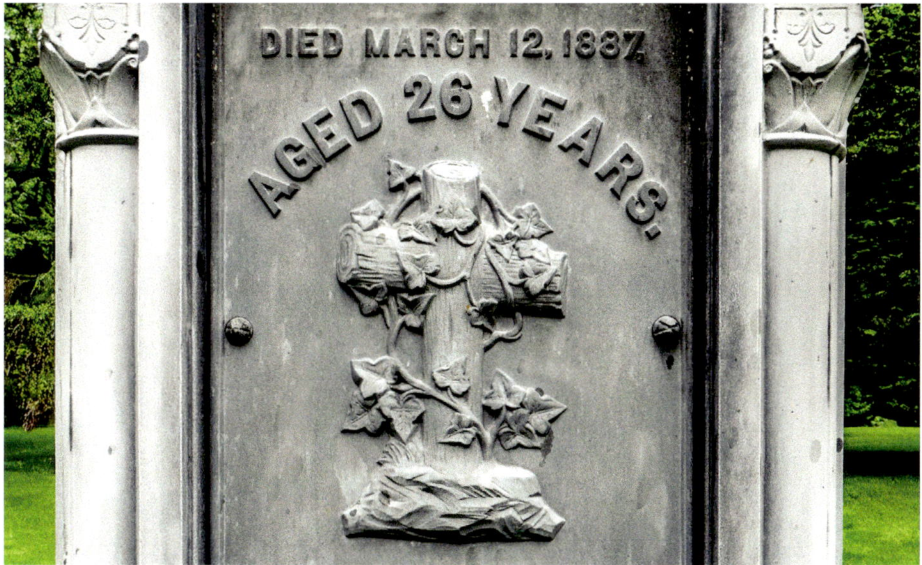

East of Rochester, the canal passes through Fairport, Pittsford, Macedon, Palmyra, and Newark, all of which have interesting cemeteries to explore. In 1828, the Cayuga–Seneca Canal linked the towns of Seneca Falls and Geneva to the Erie Canal. A zinc obelisk for Everett Van Dusen at Glenwood Cemetery in Geneva shows an early use of ivy (immortality) winding around a tree stump symbolizing life cut short.

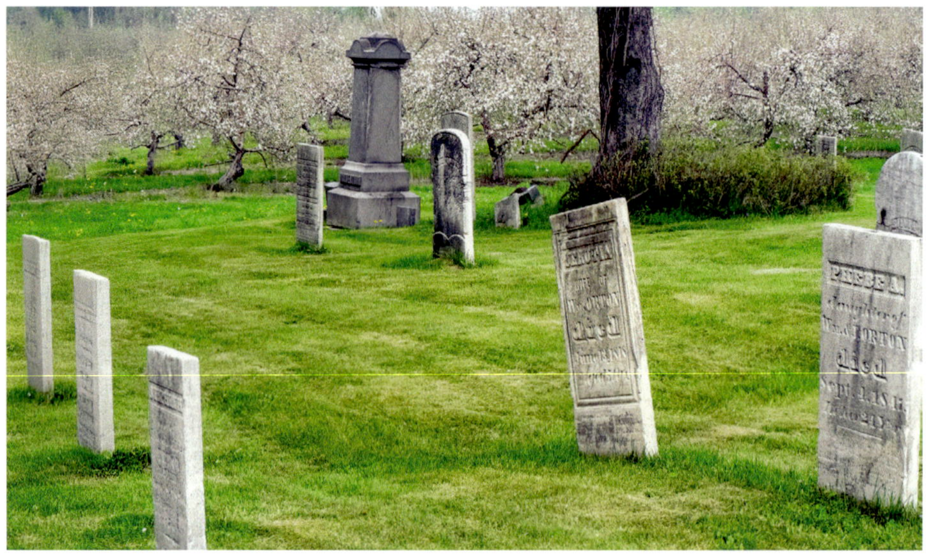

Driving along Lake Road brings you to numerous cemeteries in small towns along what I call the "fruit trail." It is replete with orchards of cherries, peaches, and apples. While fall is prime harvest time, spring also is a fine season to venture out for viewing the delicate blossoms. In Sodus, Bushnell cemetery shares its borders with an apple orchard, seen here in bloom.

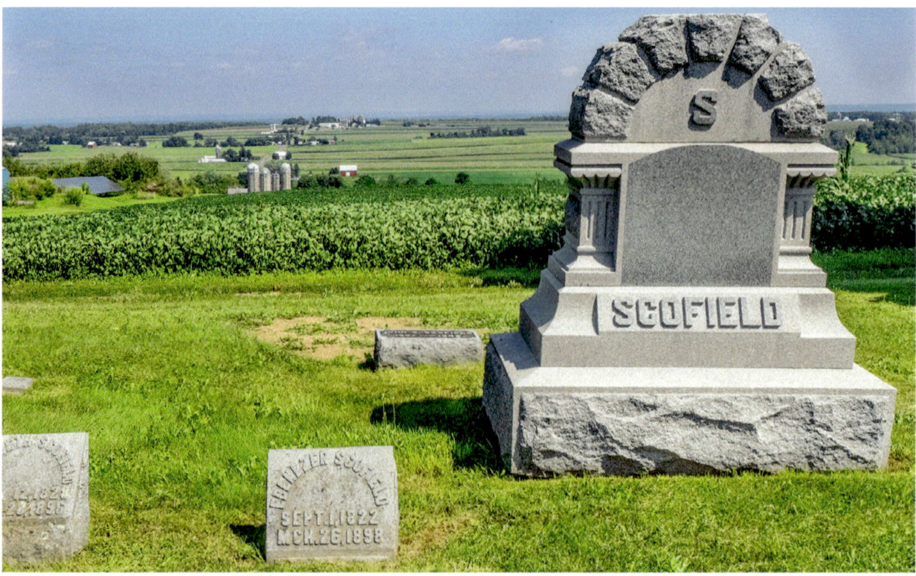

Heading south in the summer toward the Finger Lakes, many roadside cemeteries tell stories of both early settlers and their modern descendants. Benton Rural Cemetery, created in 1791, has been lovingly cared for, and it continues to thrive today. The Scofield monument is a fine example of the local transitional twentieth-century version of a classical monument. It overlooks agricultural land and Seneca Lake in the distance.

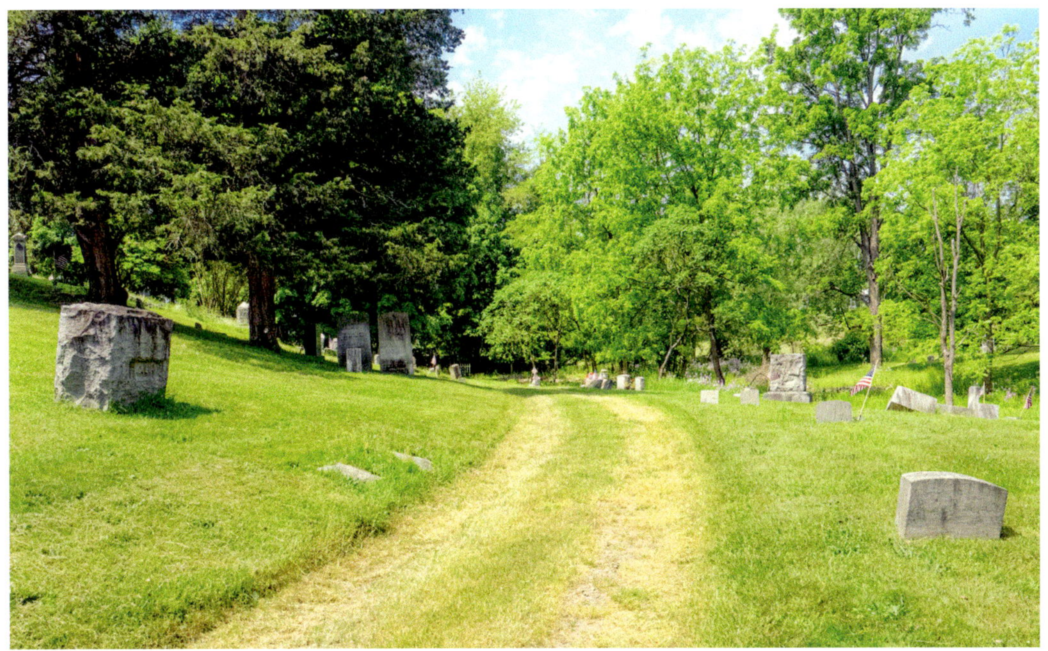

Spring and summer call for pleasant trips through the Genesee Valley. Livingston County has 136 known burial sites, enough to keep an intrepid grave searcher busy for years. Mount Morris City Cemetery is named after early landholder Robert Morris. Designed as a garden cemetery, it offers a window into the past as you wander through. Situated near Letchworth State Park, the cemetery takes advantage of the gentle hills and abundant natural vegetation nearby. Take a picnic and sit under the trees as you absorb this quiet refuge.

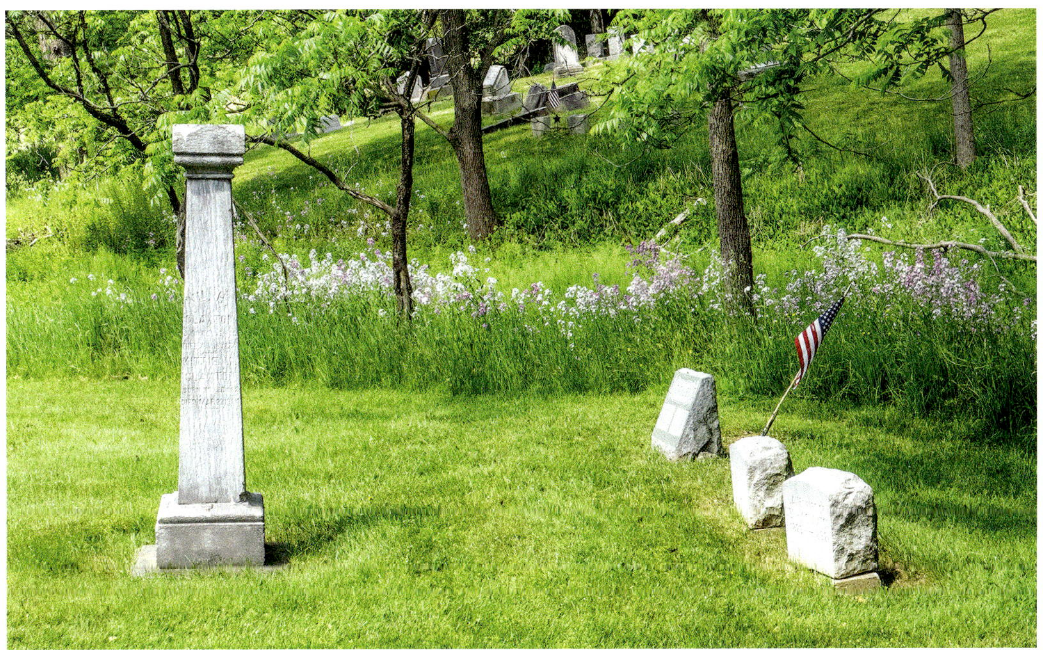

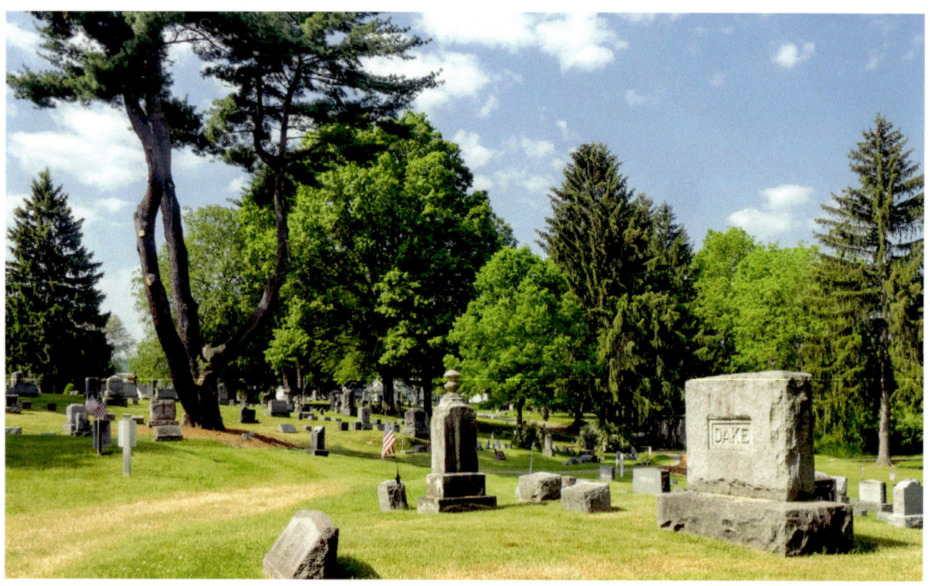

Just to the south of Mount Morris is Nunda's Oakwood Cemetery. Town inhabitants have been buried there since 1822. Local volunteer groups keep the town history alive and the cemetery in good condition. Handsome trees grow among five generations of headstones.

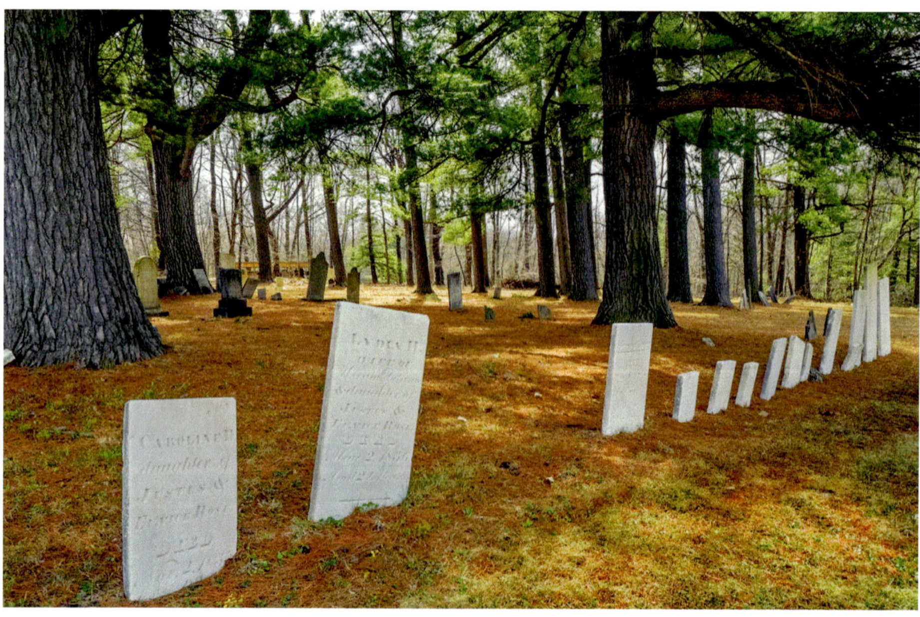

Further east, the areas of Keuka and Canandaigua Lakes are host to summer tourists, wineries and a variety of burial grounds. The small town of Cheshire near Canandaigua was settled by New Englanders and Revolutionary War veterans in the early 1790s. Pine Bank Cemetery has the unassuming nature of many early area cemeteries. Nestled in the pines, marble stones carved in New England style have survived the years.

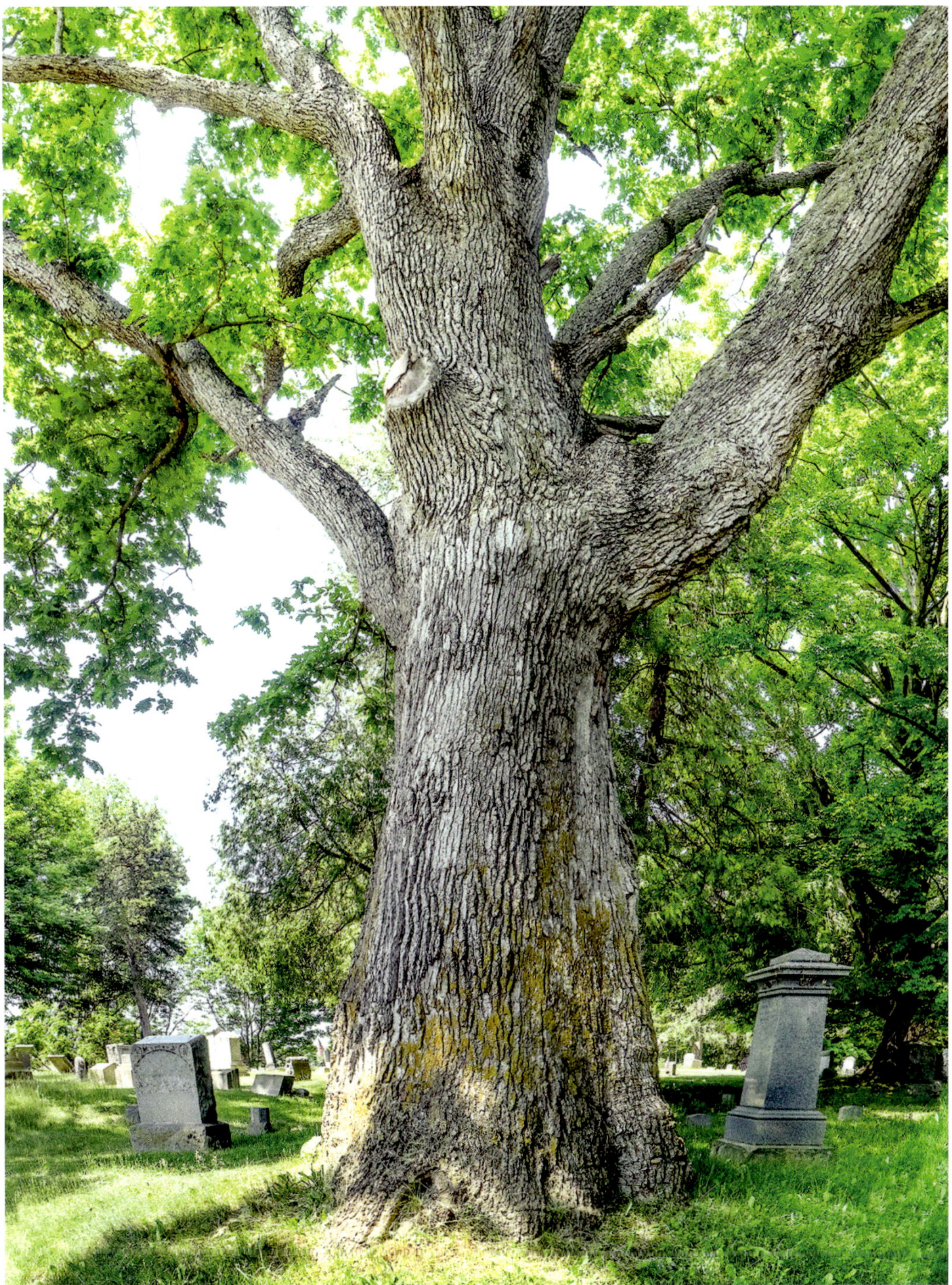

Area cemeteries host some of our most treasured trees. This one at Mount Morris towers over the surrounding headstones. Stand at the base and look up. These trees are significant monuments in and of themselves—to nature, time, and the people buried there.

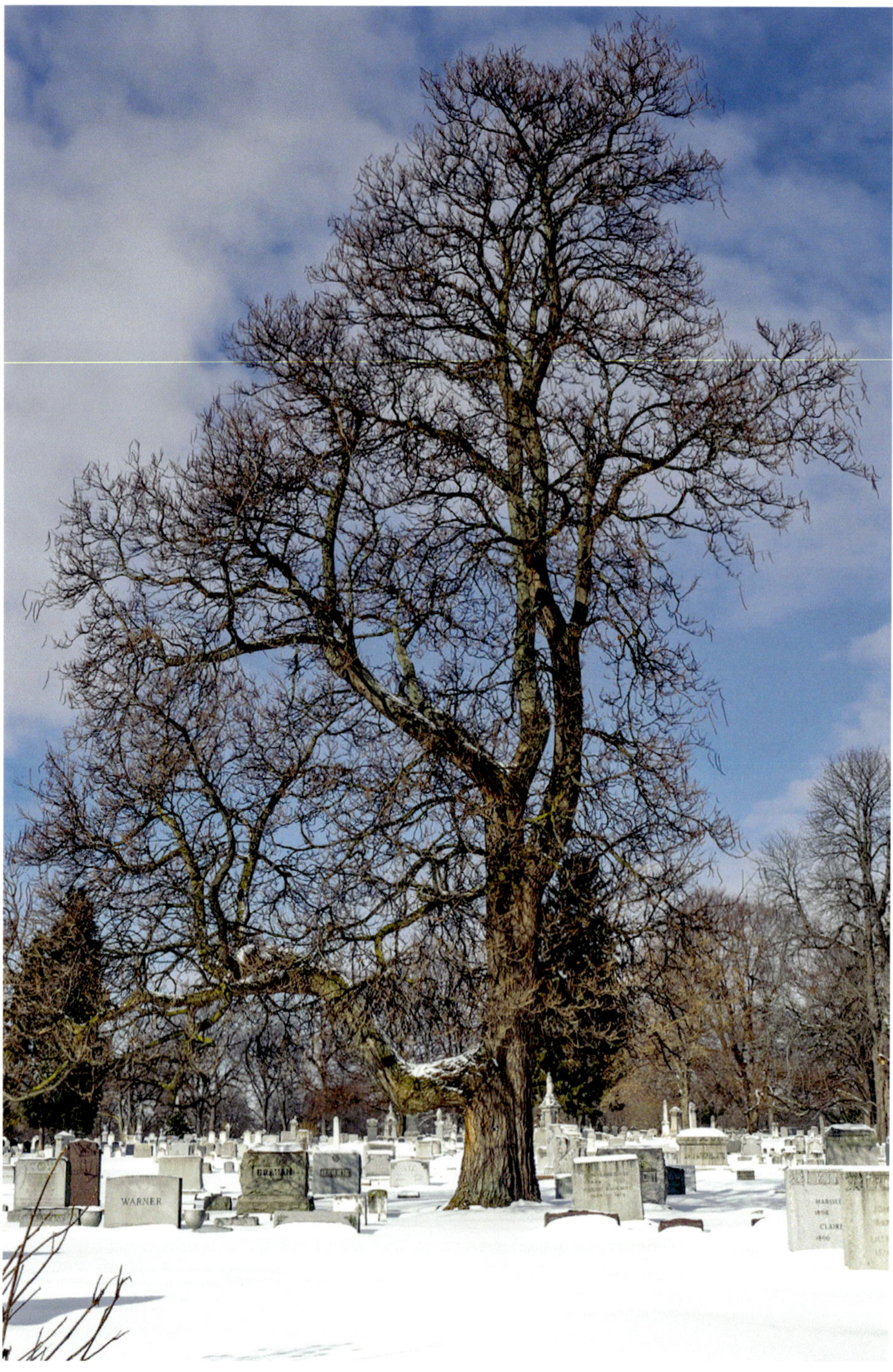

In the winter, the bare bones of tree branches mimic the skeletons under the soil. This graceful tree at Mount Hope is a work of nature's art against the blue of the sky and the white of the snow.

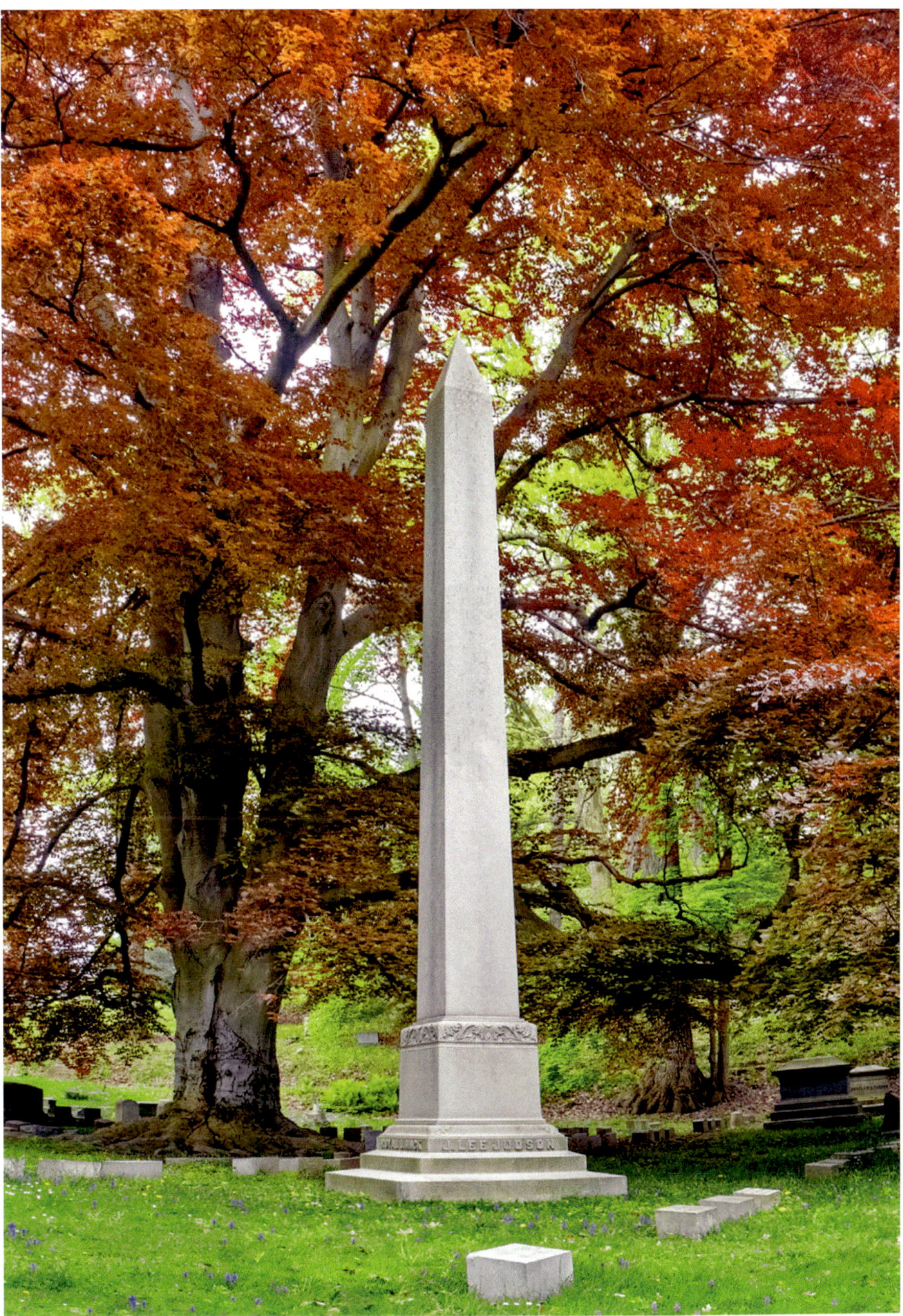

Ellwanger-Barry's Mount Hope Nursery was situated across the street from its cemetery namesake. The business grew and prospered, at one point covering 650 acres, and by 1888, it had become the world's largest nursery. In 1848, the nursery donated 100 specialty trees to the cemetery. Several of those trees have become revered sentinels, watching over the graves. A favorite at Mount Hope, this beech stands guard over the obelisk of the J. J. Judson family.

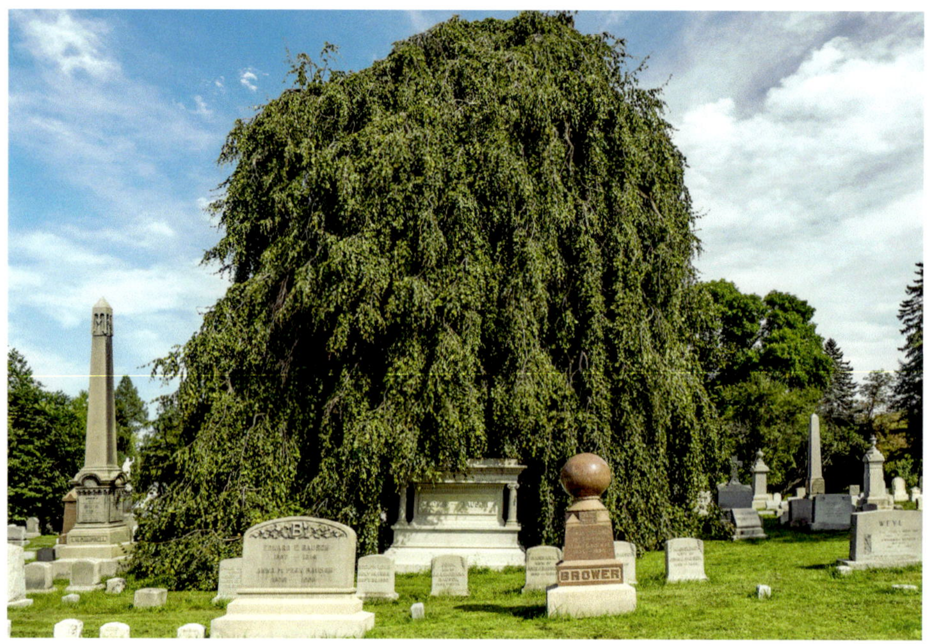

Another favorite tree donated during the same period is a weeping beech sheltering the monument for two local families—partners in business, and together in death. John Bausch and Henry Lomb, both German immigrants, created the optics tradition in Rochester, later to become famous as the Image City.

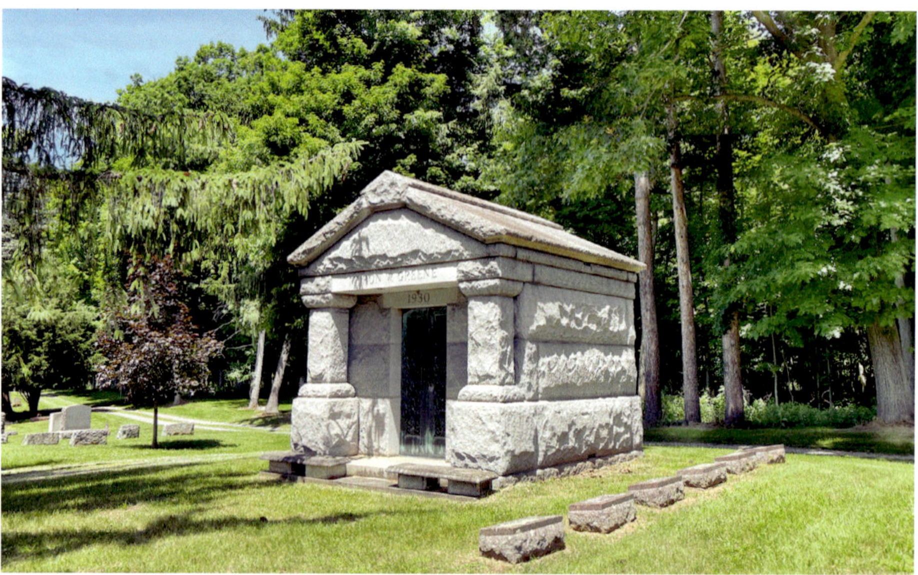

Two hundred pines were donated by Ellwanger-Barry Nursery in 1865 to the nascent Pine Hill Cemetery in Rush. The trees can be seen today behind the Greene family mausoleum at the back of the cemetery.

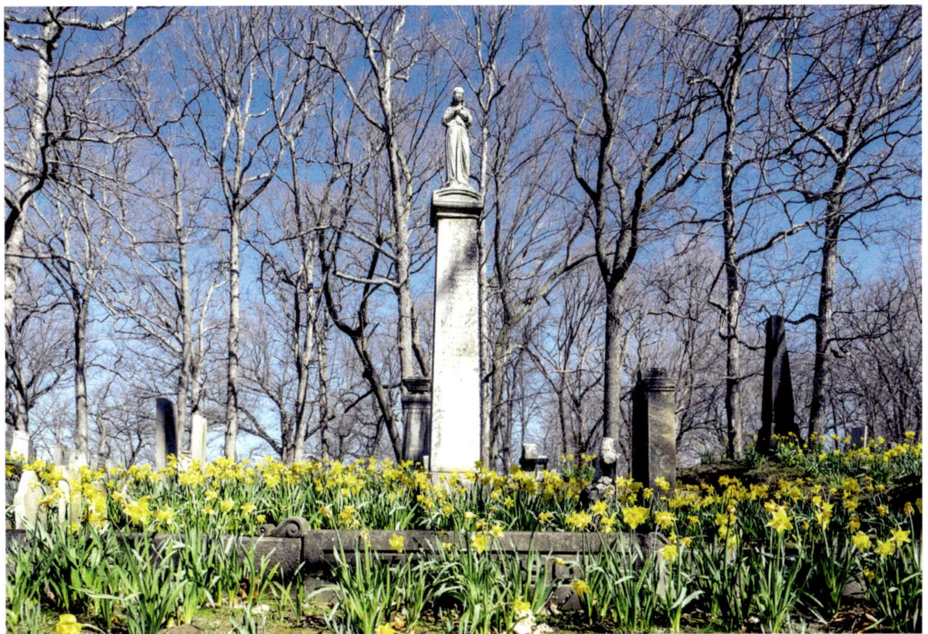

Spring brings new life to our cemeteries. Mount Hope has initiated a Daffodil Project that brings joyful color in April as we are waiting for our trees to leaf out. The bulbs flourish in an area just south of the older section where two eskers were created long ago by the glaciers.

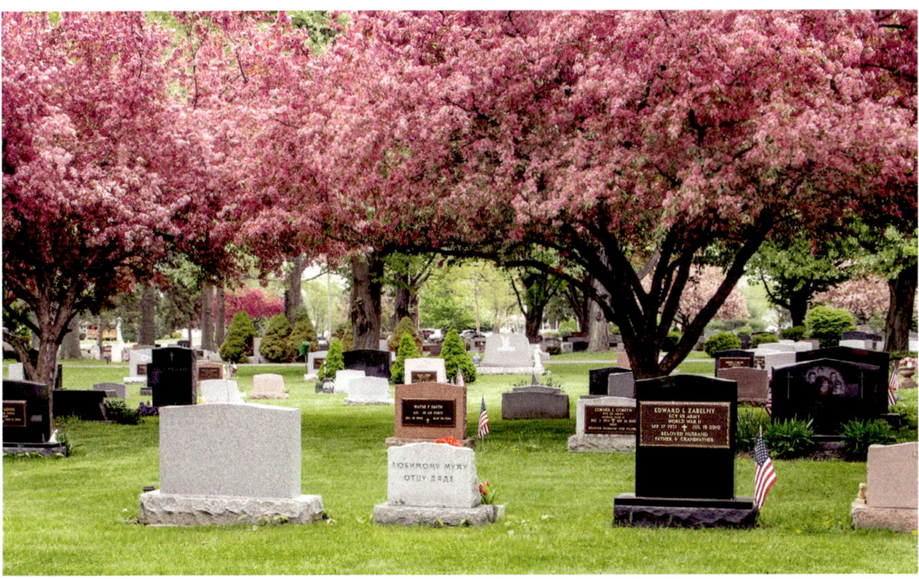

Fruit trees blossom in May. Pictured here are lovely cherries at Webster Union Cemetery. Other beautiful spots for cherry and apple blossoms include Cold Spring Cemetery, Lockport; Garland Cemetery, Clarkson; and Bushnell Cemetery, Sodus.

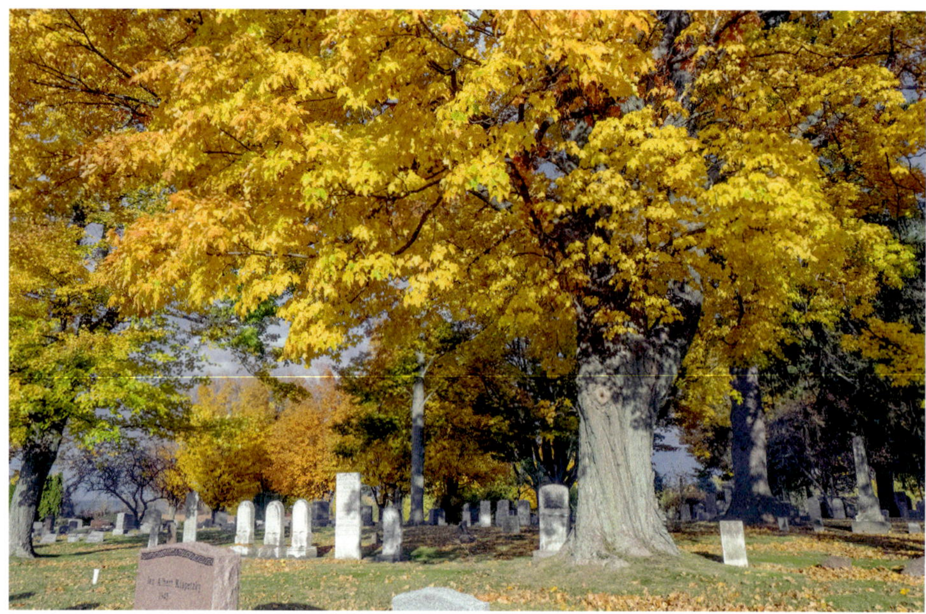

Fall brings fruit harvests along Lake Ontario, wine celebrations in the Finger Lakes, and lovely foliage color everywhere. Lakeview Cemetery, Pultneyville has grand old maples that excel at overseeing a picnic with freshly picked apples. Afterwards take a short hike to the lake at the Cornwall Preserve next door.

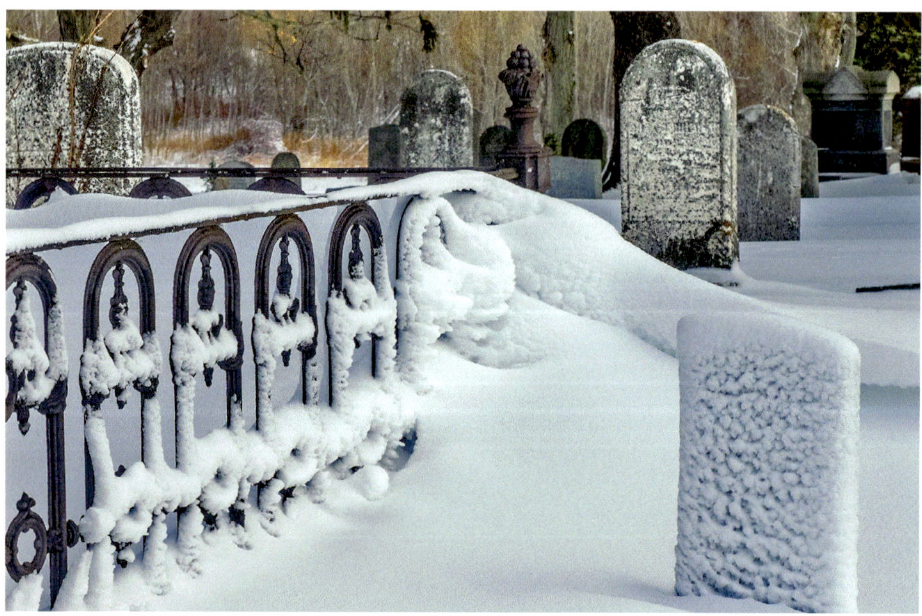

In winter, the scene changes at Lakeview to a quiet peaceful hush in the cemetery overlooking Lake Ontario. Nearly everything is serene, although a few deer may appear, and squirrels will scamper through the snow.

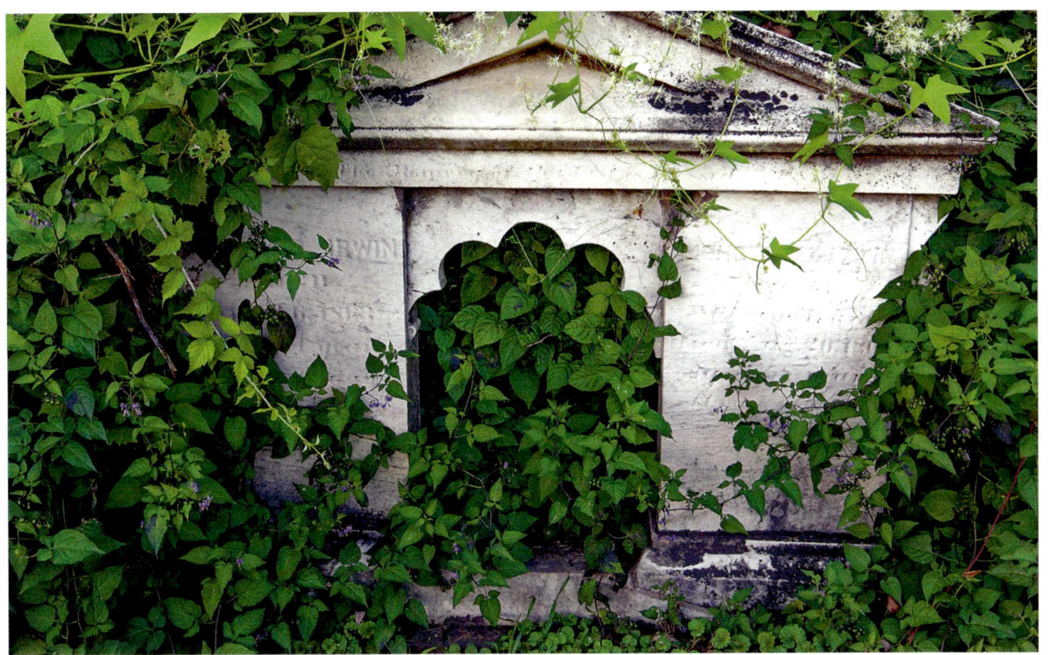

I like to think of cemeteries as permanent monuments to life on earth. The reality, however, is that monuments deteriorate. As we lose them, we lose our history. These pictures, taken ten years apart, track a rare double marble tribute to Col. William Patten Irwin and his wife, Mehetabel. Located in Bushnell Cemetery, Sodus, the image above shows that it had been under attack from vines for some time. At some point the hillside behind was cleared, toppling the monument. Today Col. Irwin's stone still stands beside its fallen lintel, but Mrs. Irwin's stone is lost behind. This dramatizes the problems of cemetery maintenance and ongoing care.

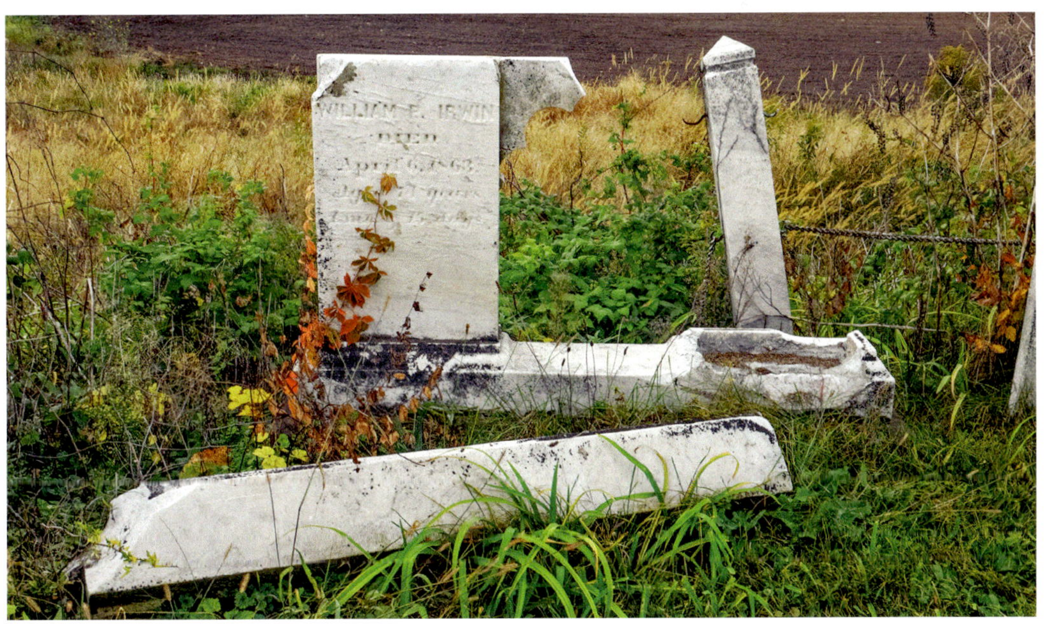

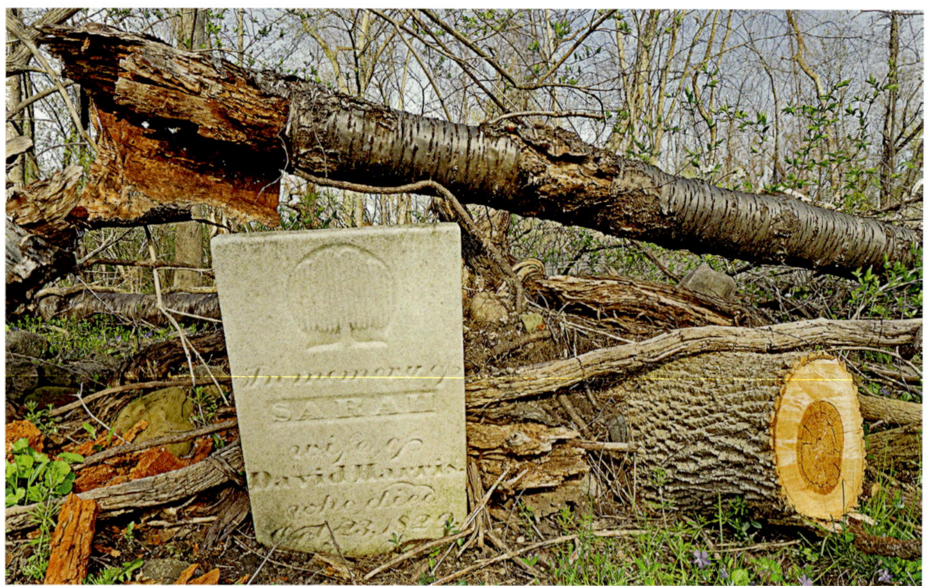

West Clarkson Cemetery on Route 104 suffered damage from falling trees. This stone escaped, but others did not. Many small cemeteries have insufficient funding to meet nature's contingencies.

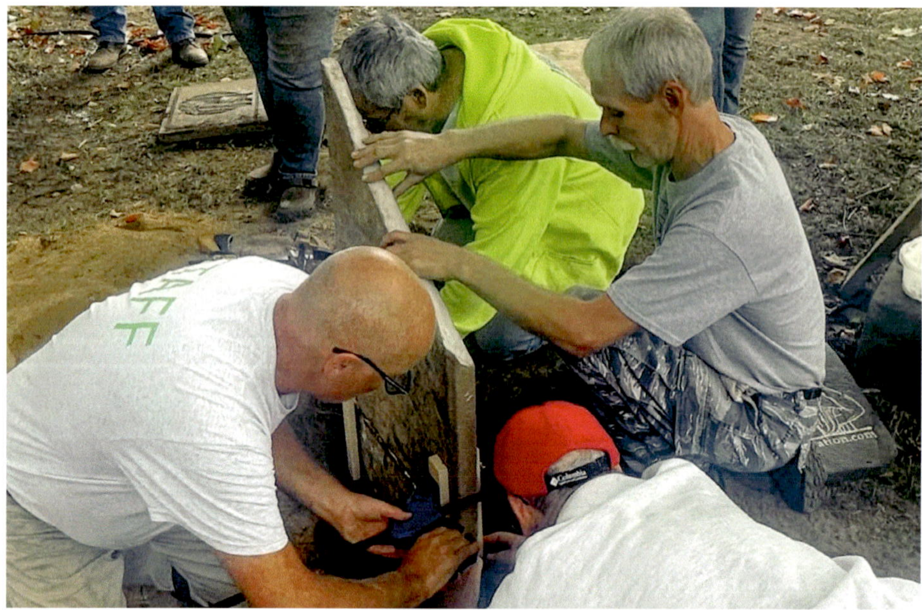

Interest has been growing in rescuing neglected graveyards from oblivion. Workshops now teach volunteers safe methods of repairing broken and disfigured stones. Recently responsibility for the long-neglected Harris Road Cemetery in Webster was transferred to the town. A group gathered there to learn from a professional restoration expert. It was inspiring to see history come back to life as several headstones were reset and repaired.

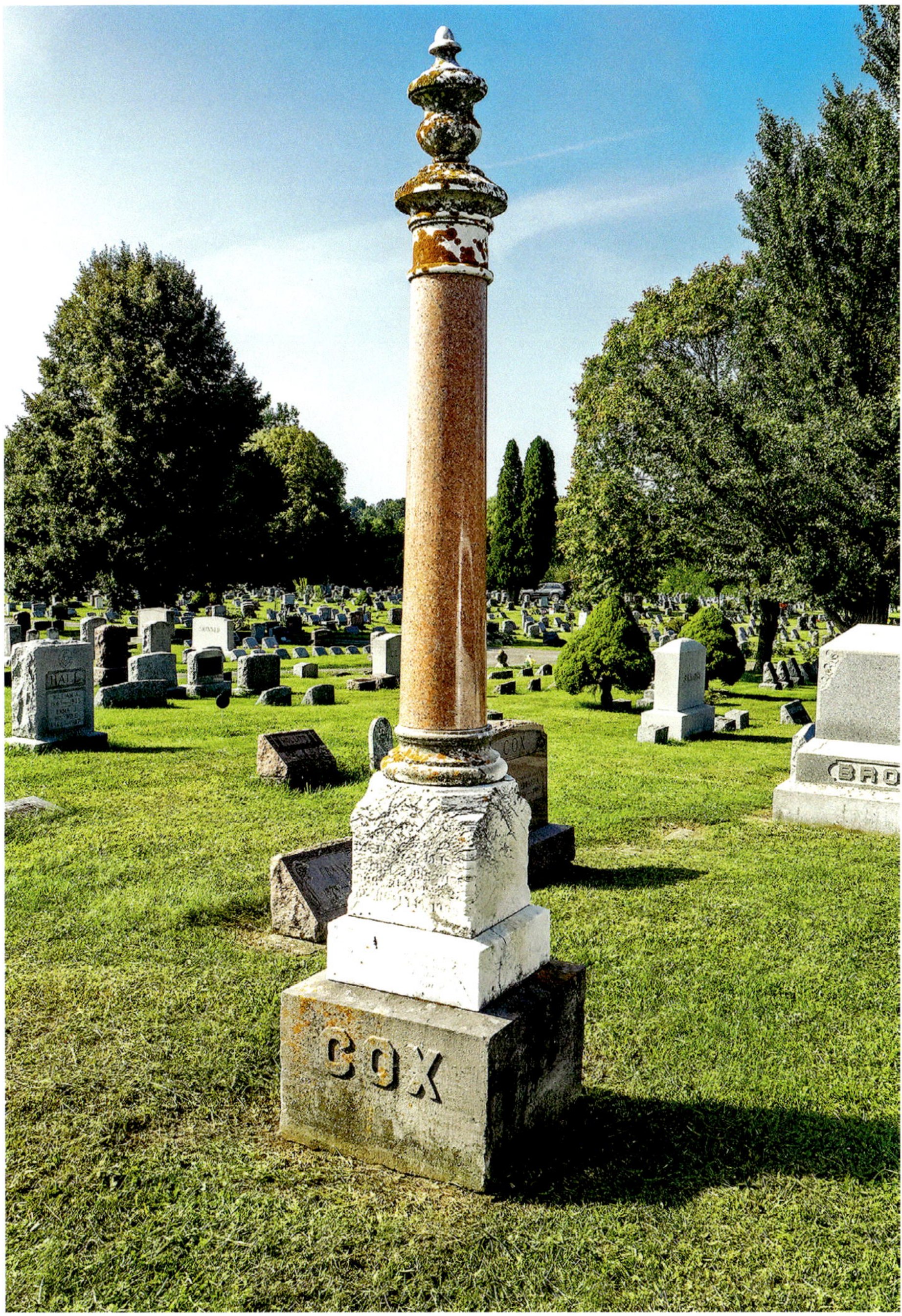

This monument at Parma Union Cemetery has been cleverly rescued from oblivion. The column has been replaced with modern granite while the base and top retain the original weathered marble. In another restoration at Pittsford Cemetery, the marble urn at the top of the monument has been replaced by a modern metal replica. Look for the Ernst monument in the older section. Can you tell the difference?

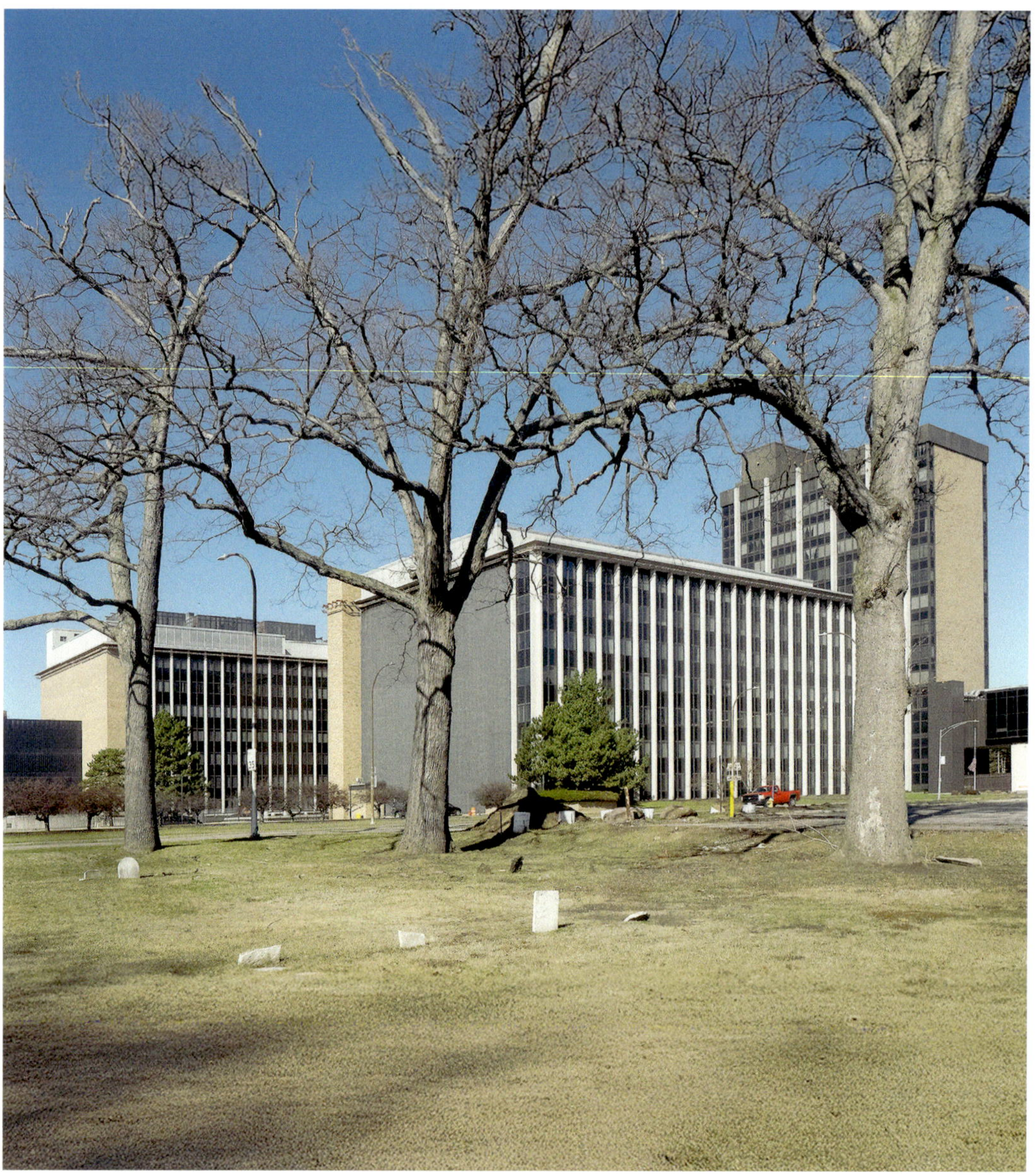

Finally, we end where we began, at Hannaford Landing Cemetery. The few remaining upright stones face another group of quite different monuments to the past—the massive architectural remnants of Eastman Kodak. The once-bustling buildings of Kodak overlook this ancient and quiet burial ground, just across Lake Avenue. There are so many stories buried underground, and behind steel and glass.

Resources

Banker, S., "The Cemeteries of Western NY Project," www.facebook.com/TheCemeteriesOfWesternNewYorkProject: Scott's organization provides volunteer opportunities for learning safe methods of restoring cemetery headstones, and in the process, helping bring local cemeteries back to life.

Bensley, T., *Boxwood Cemetery: Where the Past is Present* (Medina, NY: 2016); *Uncovering the Past* (Medina, NY: 2024): Comprehensive explorations of Boxwood Cemetery in Medina, NY, the book is locally published and available at Author's Note Bookstore in Medina.

Bernstein, P., *The Wedding of the Waters* (New York: W.W. Norton, 2006): The Erie Canal was a crucial factor in the development of the Rochester area. The book explains the original vision and extraordinary efforts that led to the completion of the canal in 1825.

Hopkins, J., *Cemetery Reflections* (Rochester: Headstone Press, 2023), cemeteryreflections.com: Photographs of 400 years of cemetery monuments, accompanied by epitaphs, prose and poetry, present a gentle view of death and remembrance.

McIntosh, W. H., *The History of Monroe County, New York [1788–1877]* (Philadelphia: Everts, Ensign and Everts, 1877): Exhaustive history of Rochester area with maps and engravings.

Parker, J., *Rochester: A Story Historical* (Rochester: Scranton, Wetmore and Company, 1884): Rochester history comes alive with the author's descriptions of our early history.

Reisem, R., *Buried Treasures in Mt. Hope Cemetery* (Rochester: Landmark Society of Western New York, 2018): This beautifully photographed and researched compilation of Rochester's well-known cemetery and its inhabitants includes a map and locations of the monuments.

Sun City Granite, "The Process of Making a Granite Headstone Monument," suncitygranite.com/how-is-a-headstone-monument-made/: The website presents a fascinating look into current methods of creating modern granite headstones.